LEARNING
CONSULTATION

GW00568080

Other titles in the
Systemic Thinking and Practice Series
edited by David Campbell & Ros Draper
published and distributed by Karnac Books

Credit Card orders, Tel: 0171-584-3303; Fax: 0171-823-7743

LEARNING CONSULTATION

A Systemic Framework

David Campbell

with contributions from participants in the
Danish Seminars

Systemic Thinking and Practice Series
Work with Organizations

Series Editors
David Campbell & Ros Draper

London
KARNAC BOOKS

First published in 1995 by
H. Karnac (Books) Ltd.
58 Gloucester Road
London SW7 4QY

Copyright © 1995 by David Campbell

The rights of David Campbell and the contributors to be identified as
authors of this work have been asserted in accordance with §§ 77 and 78 of
the Copyright Design and Patents Act 1988.

All rights reserved. No part of this publication may be
reproduced, stored in a retrieval system, or transmitted in any form
or by any means, electronic, mechanical, photocopying, recording
or otherwise, without the prior permission of the publisher.

British Library Cataloguing in Publication Data

A catalogue record is available from the British Library.

ISBN 1 85575 117 8

Printed in Great Britain by BPC Wheatons Ltd, Exeter

CONTENTS

LIST OF DANISH CONTRIBUTORS

Dodo Astrup	(Cand. Psych.)	Clinical Psychologist
Inger Dræby	(M.A.)	Management Consultant
Jan Fjordbak	(Cand. Psych.)	Clinical Psychologist
Ken Vagn Hansen	(Cand. Psych.)	Clinical Psychologist
Henning Nielsen	(Cand. Psych.)	Clinical Psychologist
Bodil Pedersen	(Cand. Psych.)	Clinical Psychologist
Berit Sander	(Cand. Psych.)	Human Resources Consultant
Henning Strand	(Cand. Psych.)	Teacher & Clinical Psychologist

EDITORS' FOREWORD

The aim of this Series has always been to help people improve their practice. Systemic thinking in itself is not enough unless it can be applied to work settings. This book is about the process by which people learn consultation; the process by which they translate the theory into the workable practice. The primary author [David Campbell] has taught many seminars on the subject of organizational consultation, and he has been struck by the relative ease of teaching—or, indeed, attending—a seminar when compared with the difficulty of *doing* consultation.

There is a Danish expression, "cheese talking", which roughly refers to the endless discussion a customer can have with the shopkeeper about the tastes of the many cheeses on display. Cheese is sampled and discussed . . . sampled and discussed—but eventually a cheese has to be selected and paid for, and the "cheese talking" stops! This is an apt metaphor for this book. How can we all get out of the cheese shop and into the real world of doing consultation work?

Learning Consultation follows eight participants from a systemic consultation seminar series as they return to the real world to try to put into practice the concepts underlying the consultation process. Each has taken different ideas away from the seminars, and each has to apply the ideas in a different working context. There are successes and failures, but there is also much learning along the way, and the reader can gain valuable insights into the doing of consultation work by reflecting on the trials and errors of others.

This book is written for anyone who wants to learn the skills of consultation based on systemic concepts. There is an increasing demand for different types of consultation—from the case consultation offered to an individual worker, to consulting to small teams, and on to larger organizational consultation. This is a time in which there are dwindling resources for intensive or individual professional intervention, and attempts are increasingly being made to help those closest to the problem to utilize their own resources and develop their own skills. This is the impetus for developing models of consultation that help others help themselves.

Readers will find systemic concepts underlying consultation clearly spelt out in the first half of the book. In fact, the author articulates the methods of teaching that have been most effective in conveying systemic thinking to consultants; but more than that, he closes the gap between what goes on during the seminar and what transfers into successful consultation work in the outside world.

David Campbell
Ros Draper
London
July 1995

EDITORS' NOTE

In the interest of confidentiality, names and details used in the cases discussed in this book have been omitted or altered by the contributors. The preservation of confidentiality is solely the responsibility of the contributors.

LEARNING
CONSULTATION

Introduction

This book has both a general aim and a specific aim. Generally—to look at the way people learn: how they are influenced by new ideas, which settings are conducive, how people learn from each other, and how they can learn from their own working experiences. Specifically—to examine the application of systemic concepts to organizational consultation.

As a teacher and a seminar leader, I have been interested for some time in understanding more about what people do with their various learning experiences in seminars. [I have chosen to use the first-person pronoun because I believe this best conveys the spirit of trying to share with the reader my own ongoing experiences.] What happens to their learning when they go home? In particular, how do they continue learning when they try to put new ideas into practice in their own workplaces?

The book is the result of an experiment. When I was invited to present a series of three seminars—the Danish seminars—about consultation within a systemic framework, I thought that this could provide a fascinating opportunity to focus some attention on the participants' processes of learning. The approach that I adopted

1

was to invite participants to write about their own experiences when they tried out the ideas. I discussed this at the beginning of the first seminar, and a few people were interested. To turn the experiment into an interesting and readable book, I thought the participants' experiences should be juxtaposed with the presentation of the seminar material itself. This should enable the reader to appreciate what and how the participants were learning and give meaning to their efforts to practice consultation. By the end of the seminars, with this book firmly in mind, eight participants had agreed to write about their experiences.

The Danish seminars consisted of 3 two-day seminars beginning in November 1992, continuing in March 1993, and finishing in September 1993. They were held in Copenhagen and sponsored by the Association for Systemic Therapy and Consultation (S.T.O.K.) in Denmark, which runs various training courses throughout the country. These consultation seminars were attended by thirty-two participants, most of whom were beginning to develop consultation work within public sector organizations; however, nearly a quarter were experienced consultants in the private sector who had participated in order to learn about systemic thinking and how it could be applied to their existing practices.

* * *

In Part I, I spell out the ideas and techniques presented during the three seminars, in order to inform the reader about the systemic thinking that underlies this approach to consultation.

The application of systemic concepts to organizational consultation results from the confluence of different theoretical traditions. From the family therapy world, systemic thinking has gradually been applied to organizational problems, particularly within organizations dealing with educational, health, or social services matters. For example, Selvini Palazzoli (1986) led a group of consultants in a study of organizations in Italy, and Wynne, McDaniel, and Weber (1986) produced a volume dedicated to different approaches to systemic consultation. Over time, as these concepts have been applied exclusively to organizational work, a body of case studies and more refined techniques has begun to emerge

(Campbell, Coldicott, & Kinsella, 1994; McCaughan & Palmer, 1994; Huffington & Brunning, 1994).

From the other tradition, the original organizational consultation world, there are a number of practitioners who have used systemic thinking in their work but have not identified it as such. For example, Schein (1987) described a new method of consulting called process consultation; Argyris (1990) used concepts of feedback and levels of measuring in his prolific writings; Morgan (1986) used systemic thinking as one possible metaphor for understanding the organization; and Hampden-Turner (1990) developed a technique for analysing organizational dilemmas, which are discussed in this volume.

More recently, these two traditions seem to be merging, with the appearance of works such as *The Fifth Discipline* by Senge (1990), who directly applies the notions of systemic thinking and the learning organization to his work.

This book, too, is an attempt to create common ground. I tried to make it clear during the seminars that my thinking and work are based on systemic concepts but that they have also been modified to suit my own constructions and to fit the work I am currently doing. I use the ideas I have found most helpful over the years. (The complete recommended reading list for the seminars is presented in Appendix A.) The following theoretical concepts form the backbone of the conceptual thinking in the seminars and are presented and described throughout Part I:

- **Second-order cybernetics**
- **The meaning of the problem**
- **The management of change**
- **Feedback loops**
- **The observer position**
- **Membership of different systems**
- **The both/and position**
- **Hierarchy**
- **Communication**
- **Systemic interviewing**

- The reflecting team
- Gains and losses of change
- Working with dilemmas
- Change and stability

Since one of the aims of the seminars was to create an experience in which participants could learn about systemic thinking by themselves taking part in the process of the seminars, I have also added commentaries about why the seminars were designed as they were and what was happening as the sessions unfolded.

Part II consists of six articles written by seven of the participants about their efforts to put the seminars into practice. Each of the participants faced a different context for doing consultation and a different learning laboratory for putting ideas into practice.

Each has described the setting in which he or she works and the way the learning from the seminars has been applied. Two work in the private sector as consultants, while the others are in public sector settings. They also range in experience, from those beginning to work as consultants to those who have been doing consultation work for some time but are relatively new to the field of systemic thinking.

The participants have highlighted the specific systemic concepts or techniques from the seminars which they try to attend to in their work, and they have been very candid about their own struggles, their successes and failures. Each has described, from a personal point of view, the process of learning about consultation.

The issues are varied. Strand and Vagn Hansen explore the risks of the consultant becoming too much "a part of the system" and imposing his own truth and his responsibility for change onto the client organization. Sander, working in the private sector, is interested in the consultant's efforts not to take the expert position while still using her expertise. She is rightfully questioning whether systemic consultants will be recognized for what they can do and hired for work. Fjordbak discusses ways in which workers can introduce consultation ideas into their work even though they have not been directly asked to consult on a specific problem. Pedersen speaks openly about pressures—both personal and professional—that may prevent a consultant from attending to the crucial process of establishing a workable contract and getting the whole organization in-volved. She, along with others, explores the dilemmas of being an internal consultant. The second private sector consultant, Dræby, deconstructs the concept of truth to give the consultant more time and manoeuvrability to help organizations understand that there are many truths affecting their problems and their solutions. Astrup honestly shares her own doubts and anxieties as she takes the reader step by step through a prolonged piece of consultation to a school, creating new interventions and exercises to deal with the changing patterns of communication in the school.

Finally, in the Postscript, our eighth contributor, Nielsen, warns the reader about pitfalls on the journey to learning and using sys-temic thinking with organizations.

PART I

THE SEMINARS

CHAPTER 1

Seminar one

I think of the Danish seminars as one long teaching event lasting ten months, but I also think of them as three distinct
two-day events, with different short-term goals for each. In the
longer view, I expected to introduce the participants to the main
systemic concepts that are useful in consultation work; I expected
to practice interviewing skills through role-plays; I expected to relate these ideas and techniques to their own cases through case
discussions—mine and theirs—and discussion and role play; and I
expected them to develop some awareness of what they personally
brought to this work.

I prepared a plan to begin with mostly concept- and skill-based
work, then to apply this more intensively to the participants' own
professional situation and do more personal work towards the end
of the process, when they had a clearer idea of what this was all
about and were more familiar and secure with each other. I relied
on the participants learning from many different sources: from me,
from their wider reading, from each other, and from the exercises
on the course—but primarily from themselves. I expected them to
play with new ideas and try them out in their own work. I also

expected them to develop their ideas and skills in the space between sessions.

A fundamental principle of systemic thinking (see Campbell et
al., 1994) is that we learn by observing and acting on the feedback
from our own actions. This is one definition of learning. Since
thirty-two people were to take part in the seminar, I would not be
able, as the leader, to give much direct feedback to each individual
participant; with a seminar of this size I design it so that participants will be giving feedback, and learning about consultation,
from themselves and each other.

The first priority in beginning a seminar is to create an atmosphere in which the participants feel safe enough to take the risks
that are necessary for learning—the risk of letting go of old, familiar
ideas and the risk of replacing them with the new and unfamiliar.

I believe that a seminar leader—myself included—should also
take some risks in order to be open to new ideas during the seminar. I therefore prefer to design a seminar by preparing a range of
presentation handouts and exercises that will cover the necessary
content but to wait until I am getting feedback from the group
about their own process of learning before deciding on the most
appropriate format for each presentation. I find I listen more carefully and respond to the changing dynamics in the group if I do not
know exactly what will come next in the seminar.

At the time of the first seminar (November 1992), I had recently
been reading the work of Argyris (1990) and I was interested in the
idea of explicit and implicit values in any organization. I wanted to
develop this idea as a major theme in the seminars, and therefore I
decided to begin with an exercise about explicit and hidden agendas. I also wanted participants to begin getting to know each other
so that they would be able to take risks.

Comment

*I came into the seminar room feeling nervous. It is always difficult
getting started, holding the mixed feelings of: "There is the potential to
create something exciting together" versus "Will I be good enough?" I
was wondering why I do these seminars and how long it will be before I
get through the nerves and relax [but these reactions are the fodder for a
different discussion!]. For these reasons, I try to avoid speaking at*

length to a sea of unknown and unexpressive faces. I introduce myself
and organize ways to have the participants introduce themselves and
say something of why they have come and what they expect. I begin to
relax when I hear them speaking and creating a context that I can get a
grip on.

EXERCISE

After my very brief, initial introduction I asked the participants
to form pairs with someone they did not know, to introduce
themselves, and then to talk together about why they had come
and what they wanted from the seminars. After about ten minutes, I asked them to talk together about their own "hidden
agendas" for coming.

This type of discussion seemed to legitimize the notion that individuals and organizations will all have "hidden agendas", but we
should not be deterred from trying to understand and work with
them.

I followed this exercise by asking each of the participants to introduce himself or herself briefly to the whole group. I asked them
to give their name, profession, and place of work, and say a few
words, in either English or Danish, about their experience of doing
consultation.

Next I gave a longer, more personal introduction about myself,
detailing some of the personal, educational, and professional influences that have led me to this stage in my career. I shared formative
experiences such as compelling theoretical concepts or cases that I
have learned valuable lessons from. I also made a point of mention-
ing a few personal things, such as hobbies, interests, or family
background, partly to make it easier for the participants to feel at
ease with me and with each other.

I shared with the group my dilemma about offering a structured
outline for the two days versus running the seminar in such a way
that we could all follow the path of maximum learning for the
group. I would try to manage the tension between being over- and
under-organized, and I recognized that participants might have different expectations about the amount of structure required for the

seminar. I put the following outline for the seminar on the board while saying that I reserved the right to shift the timing or sequence if it seemed advisable:

1. Discussion of ground rules for the seminars.
2. Identifying consultation issues for the group.
3. Case presentations.
4. Guidelines for a consultation.
5. Presentation of participants' own work.
6. Consolidating the theory and techniques.
7. Reflecting on participants' own experiences and their approach to consultation.

I led from this to a presentation and a discussion about the "ground rules" for the seminars.

I find that it is crucial to present ground rules and refer back to them periodically, to provide a structure for seminars. For example, I discussed the following ground rules with the group:

1. Since the seminars were held in English, the participants' second or third language, I made it clear that people should feel free to use Danish if they were not comfortable in English. Others in the group would be able to translate. I explained that my teaching, the plenary discussions, and some exercises would be done in English, but there were ample opportunities in other discussions to use their own language.
2. I expected participants to treat the discussion and presentations as confidential material but to share only information about themselves or their organizations which they were comfortable sharing. On the other hand, I expected them all to take some risks in trying new ideas and techniques.
3. I expected all participants to take responsibility for their own learning and for contributing to creating a learning environment during the seminars. These are not things a seminar leader does single-handedly.

4. To lead the seminar in fruitful directions, I would need feedback from participants about the progress of their learning. What material is clear to them and what isn't? What do they need to consolidate next? How is the seminar relating to their working world? Therefore, I charged the group with what I call "feedback responsibility". I have an overall plan for the seminars, but I will also adjust the direction to fit their need.

5. I expected all in the seminars, myself included, to learn from both the content of presentations and the process of what goes on during the seminars. I invited everyone to observe and comment on what is going on to enhance their own learning. For instance, some exercises are bound to work better than others, and this may become a topic of conversation in the seminar if it could contribute to the overall learning.

6. I intended to address gender and cultural issues throughout the seminar, and I welcomed comments and discussion from the participants on these topics.

7 Finally, I expected everyone to work hard and take the seminars seriously, while humour and fun would also be part of the process. I proposed to assign homework and some written work between the seminars, and I hoped that, as a result of all the work we would be doing, a consultation manual would be produced from our experiences, which could be used as a guide for "How to Do Systemic Consultation".

Comment

In order to create a learning environment in a seminar, I have found it helpful to identify the unanswered questions in each of the participants' minds. For example, I assume that they are all, individually, faced with their own dilemmas or challenges when they try to apply systemic thinking to their consultation work. If these issues can be identified, they provide the best incentive for the participants to seek out and experiment with new ways of thinking, or new techniques.

I also like to gather these issues in the plenary session, so the membership as a whole begins to sense that its own dilemmas are creating a direction for the seminars.

For these reasons, I asked the participants to discuss, in their pairs, what they felt were the most important issues to develop in order to do consulting work. From each pair, the issues were written on a flip chart for all to see, and many were discussed at length.

The participants produced the following list:

1. How does a consultant stay in the "meta-position"?
2. How to understand the organization's "hidden agenda".
3. Can we be agents of change and of "not-change" at the same time?
4. How does a consultant get hired?
5. How to understand the consultant's own hypotheses.
6. Who is responsible for the outcome of a consultant's work?
7. What are the particular problems of being an internal consultant?
8. How to identify who the true client(s) is in a consultation.
9. How to think in larger systems.
10. How does one create a willingness to change in an organization?

The next section of the first seminar consisted of two case presentations. Case presentations can be powerful learning experiences for several reasons. They can move the seminar from hypothetical and theoretical discussions to real life, which is complex, incomplete, and messy, but most of all it is the area most participants will be able to identify with. Even if they do not carry cases similar to those presented, participants will reflect on their own real-life dilemmas as presenters do the same. Consultation, as is the case with many fields of work, is learned best when the participant is taken back and forth between conceptual thinking and practice. Each should support and enhance the other.

Comment

I felt it was important to have two case presentations—one by a participant and one by me. I think it is helpful for developing trust that the seminar leader, particularly, presents his or her work with "warts an' all". A polished piece of work simply distances the participants and creates "us and them" divisions in the seminar. However, if the leader presents a case that throws up doubts and mistakes made along the way, the participants will feel more connected to the leader and more able to present mistakes of their own. The best reception for case presentations seems reserved for on-going cases for which the presenter is genuinely "stuck" and looking for some help and new ideas from the participants.

CASE STUDY

One of the seminar organizers and his colleague volunteered to present the first case to the full membership. The two spoke about the background for about ten minutes, then I interviewed them to draw attention to potential problem areas. I then asked people to turn to their neighbour to make a formulation about what was going on in the case and to suggest one intervention that they as consultants would make to the presenters. They worked on these tasks for about twenty minutes.

The case itself concerned a consultation to a school system in which the consultants had been invited in by a subgroup of the school, who were very keen for outsiders to come in and shake up the school and its management. The case illustrated several important points for the seminar. There is always an inherent danger behind any invitation into an organization: the purpose of inviting the consultant may very well be to strengthen one faction in a power struggle against another (for a good discussion of this process, see Selvini Palazzoli et al., 1986). One lesson to take from this is to move slowly and always assume that there are other points of view about what is going on and about the need for consultation itself. It is essential to consider the local, presenting problem merely as a symptom of something larger going on in the wider system.

I prefer to change the mode of teaching and/or learning every hour or so to enable people to shift their way of thinking about and experiencing consultation. This also prevents them from getting too tired. (Because of the context of working in a second language, this was especially important—the participants had to work very hard to absorb the new ideas *and* the language.) Thus, I followed the case study, which was lively, personal, and interactive, with a more didactic presentation from me about the steps in the consultation process. I presented these steps as guidelines for anyone to consider when planning a consultation, but not as a prescription that must be followed. The steps are:

1. *Referral*

   Where does the referral originate? What is the meaning of the referral for the organization?

2. *Learning about the organization and making hypotheses*

   What kind of organization is this? What is it like for the employees to work in the organization? What questions need further exploration?

3. *Design consultation*

   Clarify what the clients want. Design the format and duration of the work in collaboration with the clients.

4. *Interviewing to gather data*

   This may be an interview in the form of a large meeting or with individuals. The aim is to talk to relevant people to explore your hypothesis of what is going on.

5. *Presenting your ideas*

   There are many ways this is done, from presenting views in the course of interviewing, to reflecting discussions among consultants, to the more formal verbal or written reports.

6. *Planning and implementation*

   Presenting one's ideas is only the first step in putting them into practice. The consequences for the organization of any proposed changes must be considered as part of the consultation.

7. *Follow-up meeting*

   A meeting with the organization or the referring clients after some time has passed is a useful way to help the organization through the process of change triggered by a consultation.

CASE STUDY

Following some discussion of these steps, I presented some work of my own using the structure of these seven stages. The presentation was a single-handed consultation to a housing association going through a de-centralizing process. I interviewed each of eight "headquarters" staff individually and arranged a one-day team-building seminar for the new central management team.

I felt there were some mistakes in my work, which I wished I had not made. Briefly, when I conducted the team-building seminar there were some misunderstandings about whether I would be providing some didactic input about the pros and cons of various team structures. Also, I thought I had allowed too much wide-ranging talk about change and did not sufficiently support the Director's position in maintaining the status quo. To some extent I lost my neutrality and got carried away with the ideas about change, and, in the end, there was a counter-move from the Director. If I could have anticipated this and talked it through with the whole group, I think my consultation would have had a greater impact.

The issues of clarifying client's expectations, working through the problems of change and no change, and not allowing the Director to feel threatened were highlighted by this case for discussion. The case also introduced the subject of individuals as individuals in organizations. I felt that I obtained a much fuller picture of the housing association by interviewing each individual. I could antici- pate the effect that de-centralization might have on each and on their relationships. Sometimes practitioners get carried away with thinking of the organization as a system, and they forget that the system is made up of individuals—each of whom must be ad- dressed and understood as a part of the process of change.

I have in mind various systemic concepts that I want to cover in the course of any seminar, but the timing and the context for pre- senting a concept will depend on what happens to the group during the seminar. For example, the two case presentations stimulated a great deal of interest in the group about which aspects of systemic thinking can be utilized when working as an internal consultant.

So I took some time to present one of the key concepts for the seminars: second-order cybernetics.

• Second-order cybernetics

This is the notion that we are not merely observers of the process around us (first-order cybernetics), but that our presence and observation help create the very system we are observing. We cannot be independent of what we observe.

The main problem for an internal consultant is that he or she cannot normally step back and get sufficient distance to see the larger pattern that is influencing a problem. However, the active use of the concept of second-order cybernetics helps consultants step back by allowing them to observe their own participation in the creation of the system around them.

EXERCISE

Another way I hoped to facilitate the participants' learning from each other was to assign them randomly to groups of four. I asked them to form their own groups with people with whom they did not work and who would make a cross-section of the various disciplines and agencies represented on the seminar. These groups would then stay together for the duration of the seminars and become a setting in which the participants could get to know each other and offer some supervision for others' work, and also become a working group to practice consultation techniques with each other. I wanted to establish the groups early in the seminar to allow people to get to know each other.

When the groups had formed, I asked them to find separate spaces to work and take about an hour to allow two group members each to present a piece of consultation work. The other two were meant to act as interviewer and observer in order to draw dilemmas and learning points from the work which could be presented for discussion to the larger group.

I wanted each group to grapple with the questions of "What is consultation work?" and "How does one draw out the important elements that make a good consultation?" I hoped they would begin to think as evaluators when they interviewed each other.

In order for them to have some structure for their task, I suggested that the following issues might be addressed in systemic consultation work:

- Investigate the referral
- Clarify the task of the organization and of the individuals within it
- What is the "culture" of the organization?
- What is the relationship of the organization to the larger system?
- What is the history of change within the organization?

Based on their presentations to each other, the group discussed their ideas. They were asked to share what they felt a consultant should keep in mind when doing a consultation. These were pulled together into the form of recommendations that should be included in any "systemic consultation manual".

Comment

I often use the idea of creating a manual with course members because it puts the participants into the position of doing consultation and thinking about the concepts and techniques that will be more useful to them. Creating a manual together also encourages the group to use their own experiences as the basis of their learning and to become interested in the ideas of the other course members.

When they presented their recommendations for the manual, the following ideas emerged:

1. It was important for them as consultants to be sensitive to, and to utilize, their initial impressions about the referral process and the organization.
2. They valued a formal organizational chart, upon which they mapped the conflicts and alliances in the organization and the active feedback loops.

3. They tried to clarify the different meanings attributed to the referral process, particularly using the notion of the "hidden agenda".

4. They found it helpful to hypothesize about which individual or groups were gaining and losing power within the changing environment (see Selvini Palazzoli et al., 1986).

5. They wished to clarify the different views about the tasks each person/group was meant to do, and the formal and informal decision-making processes.

Comment

This discussion about the manual is an example of moving a group away from the content of their discussions and towards the process of their own learning. For one thing, asking small groups to give feedback to the larger group about the content of their discussions can be deadly dull. The listeners cannot connect with the experience of other groups, and they lose interest. This is a waste of time, and no one is learning; therefore, I prefer to ask people to generalize or abstract from their discussion the general principles or techniques they will use in the future. The listeners are more interested in this because the generalized nature of the discussion can include even those who did not participate in the original small-group discussion.

Following the feedback, which was put on a flip chart for all to see and discuss, I made some general observations in response to their recommendations.

Comment

I have found it more engaging for a group if I can respond spontaneously to issues as they come up during the course rather than giving pre-planned lectures. If something literally has "just occurred to me", the spontaneity in my presentation will enliven a group and encourage them to let ideas "just occur" to them. Also, teaching that is based on current discussions enables a teacher to connect with the themes of the moment and the group dynamic process, and therefore it is more likely to engage the participants from where they are in the process.

In this case, I was stimulated to make the following points about the consultation process.

• The meaning of the problem

A presenting problem should always be valued as essential information about an organization. It tells the consultant about the culture, the values, and the important structures and about strategies that the organization currently adopts to solve problems. If we utilize the concept of the "problem-determined system" (Anderson, Goolishian, & Winderman, 1986), we assume that the positions that people take in relation to a problem may lead to a rigid pattern of behaviour, which makes it difficult to see solutions to it. Presenting problems should be explored for the wider meaning they hold for the organization. Too often, consultants rush to solve problems before taking the time to appreciate what the problems tell us about the way the organization functions.

• The management of change

I have found it helpful to assume that an organization with a problem is an organization struggling to cope with change. Managers and staff usually see themselves in a changing environment—either internal or external—and they struggle to control the pace, the direction, or the consequences of these changes. In doing so they try to reconcile the old patterns and relationships with the unknown future. Questions about continued job security, status, and influence come to the surface, and employees actively wonder whether they will lose out in some way as things change. Therefore, in addition to thinking about change, it can be helpful for the consultant to discuss directly what change *means*, and what experience people have had of it in the past. For example, asking questions about how an agency has dealt with various changes in the past can lead to a picture of the worries people have about their future. I also find it helpful to identify what gains and losses people anticipate about different courses of action.

- ## Feedback loops

One of the basic tenets of systemic thinking is that individuals are embedded in a network of feedback loops—that is, people responding to what they say and do—which influences the way we see problems and organizational change. I encourage consultants to try to identify those feedback loops most directly connected to maintaining or solving the problem. For instance, I would assume that within an organization there are people and processes giving feedback that says "continue to see the organization in this particular way"; likewise, one can imagine feedback from other sources that says "try seeing the organization in a different way". Part of the consultant's job is to identify these different feedback loops, some of which are happening and some of which are potential. This has the effect of enabling the client to see himself or herself as part of a web of forces, some for and some against change.

- ## The observer position

Through a process of asking an individual or groups questions about their position in the organizational web, the individual is raised to what I call the "observer position". I encourage people to describe themselves interacting with the larger system as though they are looking down on themselves from a higher position—in the clouds somewhere. This enables people to see a larger portion of what goes on around them, rather than merely their view of the trees from within the wood. I introduce terms such as "systemic awareness" and "systemic curiosity" to encourage all the participants to become observers of the larger system.

A seminar should ideally combine conceptual thinking with technical discussions of the "how-to-do-it" variety. I left space at the end of the first seminar to pick up such practical questions. For example, one important topic was concerned with how to deal with the leader of an organization. I presented my own experiences, which are that it is essential to have the support of the leadership before setting out to do a piece of consultation. Very often the leader has given responsibility for the consultation to a lower manager in the hierarchy, but without the full support of top leadership, changes may be limited to the range of responsibility held by the lower manager. In cases where a leader invites me into the organization, I find it helpful to meet the leader beforehand to clarify how I plan to work and negotiate the possibility of looking at the leader's behaviour as part of the consultation work.

Homework

For seminars with gaps between meetings, I have found it important to set some tasks, or "homework", for the group to do between sessions. I prefer to set tasks based on the ideas and techniques the participants have been exposed to, but which allow them to try out the ideas in practice and, crucially, to observe the effect of trying new ideas. This is a way of creating a learning feedback loop for the participants outside the seminar. In this particular seminar, I asked each person to discuss with the others in their "groups of four" something they could do within their own agencies to try out some of the systemic ideas that they had experienced during the seminar. The other three in the group helped the presenter to articulate what he or she was learning and to make a strategic plan for doing something in the workplace, such as discussing a problem with the director or monitoring cases from a different perspective. I find that sharing this plan with the others in the group creates witnesses, as well as interested supporters, and increases the level of commitment to carry out the task, especially when it is clearly connected to the participants' preoccupations about developing their thinking and practice.

CHAPTER 2

Seminar two

T he second two-day seminar took place four months later, in March 1993. I was debating with myself whether it would be better to begin by looking at the participants' homework or do something unexpected to focus the group on specific themes: I decided on the latter. Therefore, I asked the group to divide equally into two groups: the "A's" and the "B's". My intention was to allow them to have an experience of interviewing or consulting to each other, and the content of the consultation was designed to allow them to explore issues that I believed would help them appreciate life in an organization.

> Comment
> *This is an example of using a structured exercise to create a context within the seminar—in this case, one of exploring the participants' own experience of being in an organization—in which they learn by drawing on their own experience.*

EXERCISE

My instructions were that the A's should interview the B's for about twenty minutes to help them understand something about their own (B's) experience of their organization or their "organizational awareness". I wrote some questions on a flip-chart, suggesting that these might be helpful in their interviewing:

1. What feelings do you have working in your organization—when do you feel most vulnerable, most competent, most competitive?

2. What are your most important alliances, your most secret alliances?

3. What are your worries about the future?

4. What are the overt/covert ways you try to influence your organization?

Comment

I prefer not to explain too much about why I have designed a particular exercise, because I do not want to preempt the participants' own experience and their learning. I like them to be relatively open-minded when they approach exercises. In this case, I suggested these particular questions because I feel they are very helpful in understanding the way each individual's experiences can reflect organizational difficulties. Some questions are more economical than others in this regard, and I find them thought-provoking for the respondents—i.e. these questions help move them to an observer position and are also very revealing in understanding what is really going on in an organization.

The discussion following this exercise emphasized the value within an organization of talking to individuals. The participants could appreciate the strategy of interviewing a number of individuals in different roles in the organization in order to put together a composite piece of the culture. In order to re-emphasize the value of individuals, I drew a large diagram on the flip chart (see Figure 1).

In the diagram, the organization is seen as a doughnut in which the individuals from within are sources of continuous feedback about changes necessary to do their work better (the feedback is

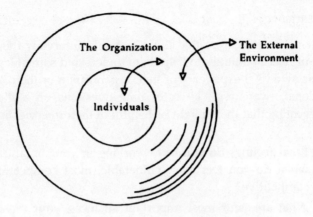

FIGURE 1: The Organization "Doughnut"

represented by arrows). Feedback also comes from the external environment in the form of economic conditions, consumer needs, legislation, and so forth, and from this source come messages about how the environment is changing. The organization is the doughnut in the middle trying to balance the pressures for change from within and without.

> *Comment*
>
> *Is there any merit in such a simplistic diagram? I think there is. I acknowledge with the seminar participants that consulting is very difficult, complicated, and messy, but it is helpful to have some basic tools clearly in mind when entering the fray.*
>
> *This diagram represents one such tool. The idea that I hope the participants will take away with them is to keep the dynamic relationship between individuals or subgroups and the outside world firmly in mind throughout consultation work. The concept is a helpful tool, and sometimes a life-raft.*

Following this discussion, I presented my ideas for the framework of this two-day seminar. I assumed that, from the work in the first seminar and their own outside reading (e.g. Appendix A), the participants now had some familiarity with the basic concepts of systemic thinking and would want to focus more on questions of how to do a consultation. The emphasis for these two days would be on my work, their work, solving practical problems, and moving further towards completing their manual on "How to Do Systemic Consultation". During the seminar I expected participants to listen to the presentations and clarify their own ideas by writing a list of "Ten hypotheses about why organizations get stuck" and "Ten steps to follow when doing consultation". I proposed to ask the participants to return to the "groups of four" they had formed in the previous seminar and discuss their homework and begin thinking about the "hypotheses" and "steps" that had become important to them in carrying out their homework. I mentioned that they would be able to return to these groups to complete this task at the end of the seminar. They spent about thirty minutes working animatedly on this task.

Comment

Unfortunately, I don't understand Danish, so there is a question of how I spend my time while the participants are working in groups in their native language. I have learned to watch carefully—expressions, movements, body postures—to gauge how involved the participants are in their task; and I can usually tell when the group needs a bit more time or has had enough and needs a coffee break. I also frequently move around the room and join a group briefly, asking some of them, or all, if possible, to speak English while I am there to give me an idea of the content of their discussions.

Conducting a seminar such as this, based heavily on the feedback from the on-going process, means I am never committed to a fixed seminar plan. Rather, I have a loose plan of areas I think should be covered in order to have a good grounding in systemic thinking and consultation. But I believe the participants learn more and reflect more on their own experience if I can fit the order, pace, and format of the presentation to suit where they are as a group. For example, if they are excited about a certain idea, I will stay with it and relate it back to their own practice, rather than drop it for another topic. Or if I feel the seminar has gone flat, I may suspend the presentation and ask them (perhaps to discuss in pairs) what would help invigorate the group at this stage.

I talk to the participants and the organizers about this during the breaks, but I also use the time while I am alone and the participants are

working in their groups to consider what is going on and where best to
lead the seminar.

At this time, I gave a brief presentation to the group about a
systemic concept that is very helpful in organizational work:

- **We are simultaneously members**
  of many different systems

  A project team in a large business might contain financial,
  planning, technical, marketing, and personnel functions in order to complete a project successfully, but there will be a
  natural tension between loyalty to the project team and loyalty
  to the beliefs and values of the function. The independence of
  functional or professional discipline thinking is essential to a
  project team, as is the interdependence of its members. Therefore, a consultant should keep in mind that anyone in an
  organization is balancing a number of different loyalties, some
  of which are within the organization, while others, such as professional bodies, may be outside.

I put what I call a "Daisy" diagram on the flip chart, to visualize
this important concept simply (see Figure 2).

The five people in the diagram belong together within the circle
as a project group, but they also belong to other systems, which
take them outside the project but are very influential in determining
behaviour on the project. For example, professional training, family
background, personality, and so forth are all parts of an individual's larger system.

CASE PRESENTATION

I asked for volunteers, and one of the participants agreed to
present some work for all of us to learn from. This participant
was working as an internal consultant in a large company. She
had been asked by a senior manager to organize a two-day management-development seminar. The company was in the process
of being merged with a larger company in a foreign country, and
as a result there was some conflict between the senior manager,

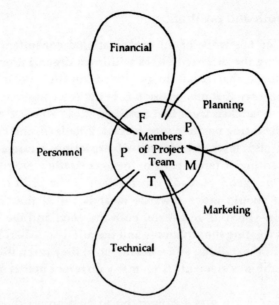

FIGURE 2: The Daisy Diagram

who contacted the consultant, and the leader. The manager was loyal to the culture and values of the company, whereas the leader favoured adapting the culture to accommodate the foreign company. The consultant's dilemma is that if she organizes the seminar to suit the request of the senior manager without taking account of the position of the leader, it will have no lasting impact, and she could become a pawn in a larger power struggle. After some group discussion, it seemed that the best strategy was to speak first to the senior manager about this dilemma. Can the consultant design a seminar that takes account of the wishes of both the manager and the leader—that is, which explores the local culture as well as the new, merged culture? If the senior manager supports this, the next step is to meet with the leader to confirm the aims of the seminar. This may have to be done with both leader and manager present. We also discussed the problem of the internal consultant. If it is impossible to create sufficient distance from political struggles, particularly at a time of change, the company may need to use an external consultant for this work.

- **The both/and position**

    Much of the work of an organizational consultant involves
    clarifying the different views within an organization, particu-
    larly those that result in polarized conflict. Polarized staff
    members see that one position is better than another; however,
    if action is taken from that position, those who are associated
    with the losing position may feel marginalized, and the organi-
    zation also loses the benefit of exploring a range of ideas
    representing different parts of the organization. From an "us vs.
    them" or "good vs. bad" construction of the process, the con-
    sultant should move towards what is called the "both/and"
    position—both us and them, both the good and the bad. This
    means creating the structures and the mind-set whereby people
    can continue talking and working until they reach the solution
    that combines elements from many different points of view.

    The case study was followed by a large-group discussion in
    which many points were made by members of the group and my-
    self. For example, we discussed the importance of addressing
    hierarchy.

- **Hierarchy**

    Although successful organizations need clear direction and
    strong management, each has its own balance between self-
    motivation on the one hand and direction from above on the
    other. Too many times I have seen small organizations chal-
    lenge the hierarchy in their organization without replacing it
    with personal responsibility and clear lines of accountability.
    Hierarchies can be both productive and stifling, and each
    organization needs to be clear, first of all, what tasks need
    doing by whom, and then to design the structure to fit the
    task.

    We also discussed the meaning of communication in organiza-
    tions. Every organization can improve communication, and many
    identify it as the presenting problem for consultants. But what does
    that mean?

• **Communication**

When people tell me their organization has communication problems, I assume several things. It may be that individuals and subgroups are closing ranks, protecting themselves because they no longer feel secure, productive, or supported in the organization. Shutting oneself off from others can be a way of protecting oneself with a communication barrier. Then I ask myself who needs to communicate what to whom. A disgruntled worker may need to be listened to by his or her boss; teams may need to share how they feel about working together.

There is also another type of communication, less personal and more organizational. This is about knowing what needs to be communicated to whom in order for a task to be carried out efficiently. In many organizations, I find that there is not sufficient discussion and agreement about how information should be circulated. I like to use the concept of "information responsibility" described by Drucker (1990). Everyone in an organization has a responsibility to pass information on to the appropriate people, and I would add that managers certainly have a responsibility to ensure that the organization as a whole is clear about what information is necessary for specific tasks. If it is helpful to think of an organization as a unified system, then communication is the glue that holds the parts together.

From time to time during the seminars, I shared experiences from my own work, and this discussion about communication prompted me to describe one aspect of some work I had recently done as a consultant to the members of a Health Service team who were having problems communicating and trusting each other as working colleagues. I was asked to organize a one-day team-building seminar. There were eight people in the team, and I asked them to form pairs and discuss ways in which each person helped *and* hindered the other in their work. Some could not think of ways the other hindered them, so I rephrased that to think of what the other could do to make that person's work more efficient. After about fifteen minutes, they swapped partners and carried on with this until all the pairs had spoken together. The group felt that this was a relatively safe way to talk, and in some cases it broke a layer of ice or two. The exercise ended by thinking of ways this type of communication could be built into the working week.

CASE PRESENTATION

The final afternoon was spent examining in some detail a case study presented by myself and one of the participants who happened to have been on the receiving end of five days of consultation over seven months carried out by myself and a colleague [Ros Draper]. This was a fascinating perspective for the seminar. I could tell them what hypotheses I was using and what interventions were made, while the participant could speak about what the effect of these interventions was and what really happened to the institution as a result of all this work. (This "happened" to be possible in this seminar, but I have often thought subsequently what a good idea it is to have a "consumer" join a consultant in presenting a case study.) Five days of work is clearly too much to present in entirety, but I would like to highlight some features of the work that were discussed during the seminar.

This was a consultation to the staff of a general hospital—about eighty-five people, representing a range of functions, disciplines, and working groups.

The presenting problem was that the hospital was going to open a new unit, resourced by existing staff, but the group was very apprehensive about how the new unit would fit in, and how the reorganization might threaten old, comfortable working relationships and plunge the staff into new ones they were unsure about.

With such a large and diverse group—from doctors to secretarial staff—it was important to break the group into smaller working groups in which people felt safe enough to cross some of the functional boundaries and explore the possibilities of change. We devised the idea of (a) mixed ad hoc groups (six per group) to which people would return regularly to build some continuity and security; (b) discipline groups (varied from three to fifteen), such as social workers, technicians, etc.; (c) working groups, which were multidisciplinary and large (ten to twenty); and (d) management groups, which meant senior managers, the executive group, and staff. This helped us hold a picture of the organization in mind but also allowed a range of ideas to be expressed from the different subgroupings in the hospital.

Some of the time, we asked these subgroups to discuss what dilemmas they were facing as they contemplated change. At other times, we interviewed subgroups in front of the large group to unearth themes and issues that may not have been clear to the group members themselves. [I refer to this as the "fish-bowl" format because a small group discussion in the centre of the room is observed by the larger group, who are then invited to comment on the content or process of what they have observed.] These interviews were conducted in a style that I call systemic interviewing.

• **Systemic interviewing**

This is a style of interviewing in which the interviewer attempts to remain neutral and open to many different ideas and points of view. The focus of the questioning is on following carefully the feedback from the client and pursuing the pattern that connects the various points of view or pieces of organizational behaviour. As connections become clear, the interviewer attempts to understand the meaning that this pattern has for other parts of the organization of the system as a whole. This is illustrated in greater detail in other writings (e. g. Campbell, Draper, & Huffington, 1991).

When groups were interviewed, we often created a "reflecting team" to comment on the meaning of the interview.

• **The reflecting team**

This is a team devised by Andersen (1990) to describe a particular type of discussion. A small group of people (three to six) are asked to observe some other event or discussion without making any intervention. They are then invited to discuss among themselves, but in the presence of the first group, their ideas which were stimulated by listening to the discussion. Meanwhile, the original group listen and may then respond to the

input from the reflecting team in any way. This is a powerful example of creating an observer position and using it to produce a range of ideas for a client to consider. The impact is the experience of hearing many valid points of view about one event.

As the consultation progressed, several areas of anxiety surfaced, mainly to do with who wanted to work with whom in the new hospital structure and how the hospital could cope with changes and pressures from the outside environment. For example, some people did not want to work with others but felt that there was a prohibition against speaking frankly lest anyone be hurt or rejected. It seemed like a conflict between respecting individuals and acknowledging that some are preferred over others. The hospital was trying to develop its relationship with administrators and politicians and was caught between maintaining the integrity of its traditional service and making practical proposals in response to the external demands.

A third area of concern was the way in which the managers received feedback from those working below: it seemed that the management structure did not allow sufficient information to pass upwards. To counteract this lack of feedback, a new group was put in place between the leader and staff to gather information, pass it upward, and comment on what they thought was going on in the organization—an advisory rather than executive group.

This case demonstrated the way in which a consultant can take an organization through a developmental process. By creating sufficient discussion, issues that were troubling the staff emerged. These were discussed at length in different settings until the staff felt that they could move on to make strategic plans for the new unit. By conducting the consultation over a seven-month period, all concerned could experience the realistic pace at which change takes place. It does take time for people to come to terms with the gains and losses associated with a new structure. Change must be contemplated in many settings over time before people feel ready to move on to action. In fact, interestingly, the first consultation seemed buoyant, the second frustrating, as though the wished-for changes had not happened, and the third was more realistic about moving into the future.

- **The gains and losses of change**

  As organizations move from differences and connecting patterns to understanding their dilemmas about change, it is very helpful to take them through a process of articulating the gains and losses, both personal and organizational, of the changes being contemplated. The tension of being on the horns of a dilemma and an airing of gains and losses produces a cocktail that helps most people or organizations move forward.

Homework

At the end of this seminar the participants returned to their "groups of four" to review their learning over the two days and to set themselves some tasks that they would complete as their homework for the next and final seminar in September. I asked them to review what hypotheses about organizations and steps in the consultation process they would want to include in the "systemic consultation" manual we had discussed during the first two seminars. They then set themselves tasks aimed at continuing their learning process between the seminars. Examples of the homework one group set themselves are:

Participant J: Would think about my role in relation to the clients when working as a consultant. Would think much about neutrality.

Participant I: Make a manual. Stay with difficult issues. Challenge myself with systems concepts. Think about the Daisy model.

Participant K: Not yet working as a consultant. Will do reading through systemic spectacles.

Participant D: Make a plan for my next consultation with a school. Get feedback about my work.

CHAPTER 3

Seminar three

T he third and final two-day seminar took place in September
1993. My plan for these seminars was to consolidate what
the participants had been learning both during the seminars
and in-between. I wanted to continue clarifying ideas, building
skills, examining practical and theoretical problems, and discussing
readings, but I also wanted to provide space to reflect upon what
the participants bring personally to consultation and systemic
thinking.

EXERCISE

I decided to begin the seminar by asking the A's and B's from the
previous seminar to talk together in pairs about what consultation work means to them personally. Why do they do it? What
personal values enable them to do this work, and which values
might lead them to get stuck? After they had completed this task,
I asked them to do a role play of a consultant meeting a client for
the first time.

Comment

During this seminar, I want the participants to practice some of the "real-life" situations that consultants have to face to get consultation work off the ground. Establishing the contract for work is very tricky because a request for consultation usually means many things.

First the "clients" were asked to give their partners—who were in role as prospective consultants—a brief or problem requiring consultation. They asked questions about their orientation, values, and ethics and how they would handle difficult issues like criticism of the leadership, equal opportunities, or staff conflicts. On the other side, the consultants were asked to answer questions but also to try to tease out why the client is asking these questions and what the anxieties are that underlie the questions.

We had a brief break to discuss the fact that the "sponsor"—the staff member who invites a consultant into an organization—may also have to "sell" the consultant to the rest of the organization. Then we had a short role play with that script. The consultant in this case was trying to understand the reason for the invitation in relation to the sponsor's position in the organization. The consultant then asked the sponsor what people felt about having the consultant come and what some of the likely responses from other staff would be when the consultant is introduced. The idea here is to try to facilitate the introduction of consultation by understanding the broader meaning and helping the sponsor to act in an appropriate way that acknowledges some of the negative as well as positive feelings about consultation.

Following this, we had a lengthy group discussion about making an agreement or a contract to do the consultation work. I shared my various experiences, and others joined in with their own. It is important to have clear agreement about the reason the consultant is being brought in, the problem he or she is meant to tackle, and the organization's commitment in terms of time and money. I have found that consultations are requested mainly during periods of great change, when many things are going on. A particular difficulty arises when the sponsor asks the consultant to provide, for example, management-development or stress seminars, whereas in fact the heart of the problem lies elsewhere—in the poorly functioning executive group, say. Because this is a common scenario, it is important for the consultant to know how much latitude he or she has in trying to tackle a problem. Can he or she look further afield, or will it be necessary to go back to the sponsor for permission if the consultant wants to look at other areas of organizational life?

Our discussion covered the need for the consultant to have a clear agreement about the design of the consultation work. For example, will he or she be doing individual interviews or group interviews, and with whom and for what purpose? Will the consultant want to read any of the organization's documents or speak to any of its consumers? It is important to clarify whom the consultant will liaise with during the work (for both management and administrative support) and whom he or she will report to and in what form at the end of the work. Finally, we discussed the value of clarifying any time constraints or deadlines for the work and the exact nature of payment for various aspects of the work, such as administrative support.

We ended this phase of the seminar by producing a checklist of things the consultant might keep in mind before starting out:

1. What kind of consultant am I—e.g. what type of consultation can I offer, what is my style and my approach, what are my personal strengths, weaknesses, values?
2. What is the meaning of the request—both locally and organizationally?
3. What kind of organization is this?
4. What is the primary task of the organization?
5. Do organization structures fit the strategy for carrying out the primary task?
6. What is the organization's relationship with the wider environment?
7. What are individuals' experiences working in the organization?
8. Who talks to whom about what?

ROLE PLAY

Having spelt out many ideas, I felt that we needed to put them into practice and that it would be helpful for the group to ob-

serve the way I might meet a sponsor and negotiate an agreement for consultation; this would then be followed by the group
doing the same in a role play. Someone from the group agreed to
set up a simulation of a case she had been working on. It involved consulting the staff of several libraries about staff
problems and rationalization of services. I acted as the consultant and began by clarifying who I thought I was as a consultant
in this context. I then shared aloud some of my preliminary ideas
or hypotheses about this case. "What did I think of libraries?"
"Did I have any previous experience of libraries as a consultant?—no." "As a customer?—yes." I shared my values and
biases, which I wanted to be aware of before I set off. Then I
simulated the initial meeting with the "sponsor", which turned
out to be a meeting "getting to know each other", rather than
negotiating an agreement for work.

I discussed with the group the necessity of taking appropriate
time to get to know the client and his or her concerns—for there
always will be such concerns—about bringing an outside consultant into an organization. I also tried to create a mind-map of
how the client was connected to the rest of the system and what
it was like for him or her to work in this library system. From this
interview, I created a picture of the culture and some of the important relationships. After a break, we continued the simulation
to design and agree a plan for consultation work. I proposed a
review of any relevant documentation, such as brochures, work
plans, and plans for reorganization, followed by individual interviews with managers and three group interviews with the
relevant staff teams. My feedback was going to be given in the
form of a brief written report and a meeting with all the staff and
managers together. I also negotiated for a four-month follow-up
at which I could visit each of the teams to discuss their progress.

This simulation prompted a lengthy discussion. A major issue was
how the consultant deals with the leader of an organization.

It can be tricky to maintain the support of the leadership when a
challenge to some of the management practices becomes necessary.
I try to make contact with the appropriate leader or leaders to discuss this dilemma. I do believe that strong organizations have
strong leadership, and I make it clear that if I have any criticisms to

make I will discuss these first with the leader and make plans with him or her to raise the issues with the staff group. I have learned from several bad experiences that if the leader feels threatened by the work of the consultant, recommendations will not be implemented.

One participant wondered how to deal with the situation of consulting to an agency who had previously had a consultant. This is often a good opportunity to build on previous experiences; for example, I would want to ask why the previous consultant had been called in and what effect the work had had on the agency. If it did not meet expectations, I would like to know why, and what the consultant had failed to do. A discussion about previous work is a chance to find out what has not been picked up and understood and thus to avoid at least some pitfalls along the way. Also, if you know you are the second or even third consultant brought in, this may be an indication that there are larger dilemmas about organizational change, so you would be advised to delve well beneath the surface to make any significant changes.

And, finally, came the question, "What can a consultant do when he or she gets stuck?" In my experience people feel stuck when they no longer feel they are making an impact on the organization. The first thing I would do is reexamine that assumption. It may be that important things are happening but that they are not noticed by the consultant. On the other hand, if things are not changing, the consultant is not introducing *sufficient* difference or the *significant* difference to the way the organization sees itself.

Most likely the consultant has lost some objectivity in relation to the organization and is beginning to accept its views and think like a member of the organization. The remedy for this malady is to step back, look at the situation from a greater distance, and introduce other kinds of differences. To some extent this can be done on one's own, but the value of talking to a colleague or a supervisor is that they can ask questions about the way the consultant has joined in the organization's belief system, and these questions have the effect of lifting the consultant out towards a new observer's position.

After a break, I introduced a session to review any of the reading the participants had done from the seminar reading list (Appendix A). I did this by asking them to pair up with their neighbour to discuss what had been interesting to them and to pose one comment or question to the large group. For my part, I gave a brief summary of a book I had recently found helpful in thinking about my own work: *Charting the Corporate Mind,* by Charles Hampden-Turner (1990).

• Working with dilemmas

I am very interested in identifying the contradictions in people's belief system and the resulting dilemmas about how to act. The inability to resolve these dilemmas is related to other dilemmas in other parts of the organization, so resolving one dilemma can have a ripple-on effect in other areas. Also, the will and energy to change cluster around unresolved dilemmas. When people move off the horns of a dilemma, it seems as though energy is released, which moves things forward.

Hampden-Turner discusses ways a consultant can work with opposites, such as cooperation and competition, to dissolve the polarity and appreciate the way such opposites mutually influence each other.

He uses a diagram (see Figure 3) to demonstrate that cooperation has meaning in the context of competition and we understand competition in the context of cooperation.

Comment
Some people learn more than others from reading, but I encourage peo-ple to refer to the reading list and get through all the texts if possible. Sometimes I make reading a required part of the seminar, but this time I did not, because the seminar was not linked to academic certification;

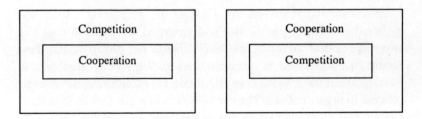

FIGURE 3: Dissolving Polarities

however, with hindsight, I should perhaps have requested some reading, backed up by requiring the participants to prepare a one-page summary of each article or book, to give them a firmer grasp of ways that systemic thinking is employed. In this case, following our discussion of the reading, the participants exchanged the names of books or articles that they personally valued and wanted to recommend to others.

EXERCISE

As we approached the end of the seminar, I wanted to ask the participants to pull their thinking together and act as consultants in their original groups of four, for our final case presentation. I interviewed a participant who was in the middle of consultation work in a local school, while the others worked in small groups to discuss their hypotheses about what was going on and to make a suggestion or intervention to the consultant that would help her develop some new ideas about her work. They did this very well, producing many ideas that the consultant thought would be helpful.

One theme that emerged from this presentation was the need for the consultant using this systemic model both to work alongside the staff and help them to articulate constantly how they saw their problems and how they wanted to tackle them, and to stay with an organization long enough to monitor some of the changes. It is a well-known phenomenon that many consultants deliver their formulations and proposals and then leave the organization to struggle by itself with the problems of implementation. In the case under discussion, the consultant had arranged to return for three meetings and was able to have a number of focus group discussions with the staff.

Following the interventions, I asked the groups to discuss together the learning points that had emerged for them during the two days and to arrive at one last question per group which they would like addressed in our final session. We had a valuable discussion about the role the consultant takes in monitoring the change process in organizations. The consultant is in a position to stimulate change but must also be aware of the need to monitor change to ensure that it does not move too quickly and frighten people back into a position of no change.

• **Change and stability**

One helpful idea from the early general systems theory is the notion of homeostasis. That is, any system maintains a steady-state of change and stability in relation to the outside environment. Applying this idea to organizations, we should assume that a change process must find the right balance between change and stability, which suits that organization. Change is usually more meaningful and long-lasting if sufficient time is spent understanding the values from the past which must be preserved as people move forward. In this sense, the consultant must be not only an "agent of change" but an "agent of stability" or, clumsily put, an "agent for the balance between change and stability". If the consultant can hold this balance in mind and reflect it back to the organization, change will move ahead at the pace that is right for that organization.

EXERCISE

The final exercise returned the participants to their original A and B pairings. I asked them to share some ideas about how they hoped to develop their consultation work in the future, encouraging them to clarify specific things they would try to do. While they were completing this task, I handed each pair a different evaluation question for them to discuss together in order to produce some replies jointly (see below).

The Danish seminars were concluded by everyone coming together for final questions or comments. At this stage, after working together intensively for six days, the group felt bound together by the experience, and the final plenary session was an important ritual for people to acknowledge what they had shared and what they would be losing as we all said goodbye to each other.

* * *

This book is about a process that begins with these seminars and continues to the on-going consultation work being carried out by the participants. As a way of bridging the gap between the seminars and the application to work, I have included here in Chapter 4 the answers to the questions I handed to the pairs at the end of the seminar. These answers are intended to give the reader an idea of what stuck in the minds of the participants and may provide a clue as to how or what the participants develop in Part II, where they describe their attempts to apply the seminar's ideas and techniques to their own practice.

CHAPTER 4

Review of the learning

O ne of the structures of the seminars was a review or reflection period following each input or exercise so that the participants could consolidate their learning or simply take stock of what had been happening to them. On this basis, I also wanted them to have an opportunity to review their learning over the duration of the seminars. I prepared seven questions—one for each discussion group—and asked them to discuss together their responses to the questions. The questions and replies are presented in this chapter.

However, the chapter is also intended as a transition. It highlights some of the experiences or ideas people took away from the seminars and anticipates how they might develop their learning about consultation further—once they were working on their own. The questions were designed to enable participants to review the past ten months of the seminars as well as their own attempts to put things into practice; however, the real proof of this pudding becomes more clear in the "eating" of case studies presented by the participants in Chapters 5–10.

The seven questions are as follows:

1. **What specific things do I do differently now in my consulta-**
   tion work?

- *I dare to be more aware of the present—and less "prepared". Let things*
  be said without feeling that I must do something with it. Let it belong
  to the group.
- *I have gained much more awareness of the individual's role and needs*
  in the organization, thus becoming more supportive of dilemmas aris-
  ing from membership of different subsystems.
- *I am much more comfortable in the role of being insecure/uncertain*
  when things are happening in the group process, and consequently I
  can more quickly go back to the state of being curious.
- *Take more time to clarify the contract.*
- *Be aware not to take away the responsibility from the client.*
- *Point out dilemmas.*

2. **What's the most important way my understanding of consulta-**
   tion has changed?

- *Remember the leader.*
- *Give yourself time—go slow.*
- *Be aware of not taking responsibility for the organization's problems.*
- *Do not seek to understand everything.*
- *The initial contact and exploration of the meaning of the referral is*
  extremely important.
- *Clarify the contract—what you are supposed to do and whether you*
  want to do it.
- *Attention to process and receiving feedback.*
- *The personal meanings of any discrepancy between the individual and*
  his or her role.
- *Not to think you know better, while acknowledging that you do have*
  special knowledge.
- *To create a process with space for reflection and time for learning points*
  for the participants and the consultant.

3. **What were the three most helpful** *skills* **you have acquired for doing systemic consultation?**

- *Taking a position of being empathic, listening, understanding, curious.*
- *Accepting and starting with the description of the situation that the clients put forward.*
- *Achieving knowledge of different organizational structures and transforming this into action.*
- *Being aware of the deliberate pace in the process of creating the initial contract and speaking to each level in the organization.*
- *Conducting the initial interview and making the contract clear.*
- *Exploring hierarchy and other organizational structures.*

4. **What were the teaching techniques during this seminar which were most helpful for your learning about consultation?**

- *Creating a situation with direct feedback from role-play clients after the simulations and role plays.*
- *Training with role plays, concrete situations, and the mix with reflecting teams.*
- *Moving back and forth between theory and practice.*
- *Presenting of cases and giving/getting feedback.*
- *Shifting between giving theoretical input and taking the observer's role.*
- *Making learning points after each exercise.*

5. **What were the most important parts of the process of learning consultation?**

- *Specific tools (things to be said, questions to be asked, groups to be formed) that I believe I will remember while doing consultation work and more readiness to look for the "rationale" in the client belief system, rather than in my own.*
- *The connection between theory, practical advice, and the different cases that were presented. It gave a feeling of understanding the very complex material, so it was possible to adapt it a little more easily to work.*

- *There were some specific tools (what to do if/when you are in a specific situation)—but most of all there were the unspecific sediments left on the beach by a lot of waves.*

6. What has the experience of this seminar taught you about "learning"?

- *I have been able to be more conscious of my own thinking by comparing it to many different ways of thinking.*
- *The surprise that it is possible to learn from others in a big group— without a group-development phase (there were few efforts to develop the group).*
- *The importance of creating a safe atmosphere—for example, sharing our own experiences and insecurities.*
- *The importance of an on-going group: it stimulates experiments and learning between meetings.*
- *Make a clear frame for each unit of time during the seminars.*
- *To get the learning points out of each conversation/consultation and then to think about "then what" and "both/and" and "gains and losses".*
- *To get the context/contract clear. Not to rush.*
- *The necessity of feeling free to take a consultation job or not.*

7. What would be the next stage for my learning about consultation?

- *To read more.*
- *To create new settings in order to ask for feedback (supervision, work with colleagues, etc.).*
- *Planning and carrying out interventions and the possibility of trying them out in role plays with particular subgroups of the institution.*
- *Experimenting with different interventions in the same system.*
- *To turn consultancy jobs into cases to be used in a book.*

PART II

THE APPLICATIONS

CHAPTER 5

Should consultation fit the client's expectations?

Henning Strand & Ken Vagn Hansen

INTRODUCTION

Working as co-consultants, we have gradually changed our method from a very structured process planned in every detail to a much more process-oriented style creating new feedback within the organization.

In this chapter we present our experiences of learning about process consultation as new consultants in this field.

Both of us are experienced clinical psychologists employed by the county. Our job is mainly to serve schools and day-care institutions. We offer supervision to teachers, do psychological evaluations of children, and also do individual and family therapy at the clinic. We are both interested in the systems around clients. For instance, we offer consultations to families and the professional system around the families.

Because of the interest in consultation, we have occasionally been contacted by staff members of a school or a high school who needed help to improve their working relationship.

As we find it challenging to deal with larger and more complicated systems, we have accepted the invitations and have worked with whole staffs of teachers and leaders (40–70 persons).

OUR VALUE SYSTEM

We now see that we have generally been organized by the belief that if we negotiated the conditions and goals of the consultation with the management without staff participation, this might result in insecurity and resistance among the staff and impede future progress.

Obviously this belief has something to do with our view of democracy in organizations, but it also has to be understood in connection with the very flat hierarchy of Danish educational institutions, in which the staff expect to participate in any discussion about changes.

Our intentions to ensure that the staff were always represented when we negotiated the conditions of the consultation encouraged us to remain neutral between the management and the staff; in retrospect, however, this may have induced a sense of insecurity in the management about our neutrality; we elaborate on this later in the chapter.

DEVELOPING A NEW METHOD

Requests from the school have shown that both the leaders and the staff were very aware of the structure and the content of the organization and were preoccupied with changing the structure. However, they showed very little interest in the process—that is, anticipating the consequences of possible changes for the individual and for the organization.

In our first consultations, we responded to these expectations that the structure had to change, especially because we ourselves needed a structure that could make it easier for us to cope with our own insecurity. But it soon became apparent that by working in such a structured way we lost the opportunity of focusing on the current changes in the system and of figuring out what these changes meant to the participants and to the organization. Eventu-

ally, our therapeutic experiences, coupled with the Danish seminars, led us to change our consultation style.

Primarily, we started to reflect on the consultation process in
front of, and together with, the participants as a part of the process.
In addition, we started to pay a great deal more attention to feedback from the consultees. In other words, we became more process-
oriented. Working as co-consultants, we thus gradually changed
our method from a very structured programme planned in every
detail and starting with a certain way of presenting the problems, to
a much more process-oriented style creating new feedback within
the organization.

We now see ourselves as feedback agents, which means that the
aim in our consultations is to utilize the feedback in the system. The
idea of focusing on the feedback processes comes from the assumption that the information you need to understand the constraints
and possibilities of development in an organization has to be
shared and connected in order to facilitate organizational change.

We endeavour to increase and to stimulate feedback by creating
a context in which different views and expression of the relations in
the organization are accepted and where consideration is shown for
individual needs for stability or growth.

By being explorative, curious, and respectful to all the participants, we try to take a meta-position from which we can observe
the process without taking sides. We endeavour to turn questions,
dilemmas, and confusions back to the organization instead of
blocking the process by offering quick interpretations. In this way,
the participants have the chance to find several alternative meanings and eventually to construct new connections and thus new
insights. By showing respect for all points of view and accepting
several different or even contradictory ideas at the same time, we
avoid on a large scale the resistance of the participants that follows
from a feeling of not being heard.

Despite all these advantages, we nevertheless find it both difficult and challenging to do consultations in which the process is
clarified by utilizing feedback. It is difficult because we have to
cope with the insecurity of being in the process, not knowing what
to do next and without the safeguard of a programme prepared in
detail. But it is also challenging and, paradoxically, secure because

we know that we can achieve further progress by putting the dilemmas and the confusion back into the organization and thus sharing with the consultees the responsibility for any outcome.

In other words, we intervene in the process by extemporizing from the continuous feedback between the participants, between the participants and the consultants, and between the consultants.

To work with feedback processes as a method means that we as consultants have to be ready to take the consequences of the feedback we receive—that is, to let go of any hypothesis that is not met with sympathy by the participants and to find an alternative hypothesis. In other words, we have to be ready to change, to be open-minded to alternative views in the same way as we expect the participants to use the feedback to develop new understandings and new ideas.

As mentioned, we do not have a great deal of experience with process consultation, so we still feel a rush of adrenaline in the blood when—even though we still have no specific ideas about the next step—we have to make reflections in front of a large group of consultees who are expecting us to know what is going to happen.

By taking feedback from the participants seriously, by staying strictly to the subject, and by reflecting about the dilemmas in a situation that has reached a deadlock, it has been possible for us and for the participants to understand new aspects of the relations in the organization and to make further progress.

JOINING THE TRAINING GROUP
IN CONSULTATION

Having done a few consultations together, we formed a peer group at our working place for mutual support and for peer supervision on our consultation work. The group consisted of five psychologists. Our intention was to try to understand and to learn from the difficulties we met during the consultations.

However, the peer group turned out to be of limited value because our three colleagues were very preoccupied by structure, content, and goals whereas we needed help to focus more on the *process* of our consultations.

Because of this desire to be more clear about our own way of doing consultation and a need to achieve new skills, we joined the Danish seminars. During these seminars we presented a case for discussion and supervision. The case is about a consultation at a high school; we started a month before the seminars began and were still working on it at the time of the second seminar.

We presented the case in the training group because we were uncertain about the course of the consultation, and how the participants experienced the consultation, since there was a total lack of response from the headmaster when we asked him for an evaluation meeting. We needed the training group to help us to understand this situation and to suggest what to do.

The supervision we received in the training group centred around the contract we had made with the leader and the contact person and, especially, our failure to understand the importance of the role of the leader. We now see that because we soon came to regard him as a weak leader. we might not have shown him sufficient respect, He might have felt our perception of him and begun to doubt that we really wanted to understand his position and that he could feel secure about our work as consultants.

CONSULTATION AT A HIGH SCHOOL

We were initially contacted by one of the teachers, who knew a colleague of ours. This teacher presented a need for help with some staff collaboration problems at the high school. She was in direct contact with the headmaster, and it was our impression that she wanted to help him to find a way of overcoming these problems. They did not have any previous experiences of consultation.

We asked for a meeting with the teacher and the headmaster. This was the first step in the following consultation.

1. *The meeting between the two of us and the headmaster and the contact person.*

We asked why they had contacted us, what they expected from us, why now, and so on.

They told us that the high school had about 700 students and 70 teachers. They described the school as having good success with the students in comparison with other schools. But there were some pressures from the outside and some conflicts on the inside.

They were forced to make budget cuts and had to dismiss some teachers. The morale of the teachers was low at times. They had difficulties in making decisions, because there were some strong groupings of teachers who would not compromise. The headmaster expressed his dissatisfaction with the discussion structure. He wanted to be more able to handle conflicts and for there to be a stronger team spirit. The headmaster and the contact person thought that there could be some resistance to the consultation from a group of teachers who would have "a superior academic attitude" towards us—they had seen that before, they told us.

After the meeting, we considered the referral to us and made hypotheses about intentions and views and also about power in the organization, hidden agendas, problems, and possibilities.

However, we needed another meeting because the headmaster was not yet ready to make a final contract with us at this moment. We think the headmaster was somehow uncertain and insecure about what kind of "help" we could offer and about the risk posed to him by our consultation. We saw him as a rather weak leader, and perhaps he sensed our scepticism.

One thought that emerged from the training seminar was to give more attention to the leader, and we decided to offer a follow-up meeting with the headmaster.

2. *Another meeting between the four of us.*

We asked more about the headmaster's views on the situation in the organization, the structure, values, and so on; and we explored his needs.

At the meeting, we proposed that he should invite delegates from the staff to a third meeting so that we could have the opportunity to get an impression of how a broader group in the staff understood what was going on in the organization, how they saw the needs of the organization, and what they wanted and expected from us.

Our purpose in proposing this meeting was to make a contract with the headmaster and the delegates from the staff group about time, purpose, and aims.

We have subsequently reflected on this step in our consultation, and we see it now as a sign of *our* need to have a kind of contract

with all participants, and also an expression of a democratic attitude from our side—a wish to "take care" of the staff at the
"grass-roots" level. This step was perhaps the first sign of a fundamental problem in our consultation.

3. *A meeting with the contact person, the headmaster, and a group of
    teachers chosen by the staff and the leader.*

We asked again about their expectations. Also, at this meeting we
were very careful not to make alliances with anybody, and we
asked a lot of questions to find out why we had been invited, why
now, who had had the idea, what was changing in the organization,
how they reacted to these changes in the organization, what they
expected from us, what resistance we could expect, and so on.

Even though we paid a lot of attention to observing our own
position and function in the system, afterwards we could see that,
in many ways, we had become trapped by the organization. (We
return to this later in the chapter.)

The impression gradually formed in our minds that the organization had a leadership problem: the headmaster was insecure about
how he should handle the different tensions in the organization.

There were groups of old and new teachers, each of which had
its own views on how to develop the school; there were different
professional groups of teachers who had much power; and so on.
We discovered that the headmaster was very isolated and that he
had difficulty handling all these differences. The headmaster had
found a support in the contact person, and they hoped that we
could do something without the headmaster being criticized even
further because of his decision to hire us.

It was our impression that the climate in the organization was
characterized by lack of communication across and between the
groupings. Our hypothesis was that people were insecure and defensive, which made them criticize the headmaster and seek comfort in the different groupings.

The conditions of the consultation day had been settled in advance: the entire staff (70 teachers) was expected to participate, and
a certain amount of time was allocated.

In this situation, we decided to design a consultation that involved everybody and in which our aim was to create a more open
and listening atmosphere.

4. *Agreed by the headmaster and the delegates, we send an introductory letter to all the teachers.*

In the letter, we briefly introduced ourselves, mentioned the agreement, and explained the concept of consultation.

5. *A meeting with the headmaster and the contact person at which our thoughts about the structure of a "consultation day" was explained.*

6. *The consultation day and a short meeting afterwards with the headmaster and the contact person.*

The consultation day

1. *Everybody met in the teachers' staff room for a cup of coffee. The headmaster gave a short introduction to the day. Everybody went to the main room.*

2. *All the teachers were seated in a large circle. We introduced ourselves, and Henning made a short presentation of our method of working (our ideas about feedback; use of reflecting teams; hypotheses; helping the participants to observe themselves and the other in the organization; understanding differences on a higher level; making connections; and so on).*

3. *In order to make a connection between our meetings with the headmaster and the contact person and all the other participants, we arranged an interviewing group and a reflecting team in the middle of the circle.*

The interviewing group consisted of the contact person and the headmaster, and they were interviewed by Henning. He asked them who had decided to ask for a consultation, how the teachers were informed, and how they had responded to it. He also asked the pair what they expected to achieve, and what expectations they thought the teachers had about the consultation.

The members of the reflecting team were selected randomly, and the reflections were conducted by Ken. This group reflected on the interview in the other group.

4. *We next asked everybody to form pairs by wandering around among each other to find the person they knew the least.*

Asking them to select an unfamiliar partner was a way of making it easier for them not to take too much for granted and to remain curious during the interview.

The pairs were given a written task. We asked them to reflect over their working situation singly and, afterwards, to interview each other about their reflections.

We asked them to think individually about what they would like to be different about cooperation at the high school in the future, and what they wanted to preserve as it was then. They were then asked to reflect over what they wanted to get out of this day.

We also asked them to reflect over their hidden agendas for this consultation day and to share some of them with their partner.

5. *Then the pairs met in the main room. They were asked to wander around among the other pairs and choose another pair. Each group of four found a working place.*

They shared within the individual subgroups the central points in their interviews. After this sharing, they were to make a synthesis of the points and write this on a sheet of flip-chart paper.

Our purpose of the instruction about synthesis was to give the single participant the opportunity to put his or her point of view on a higher systemic level.

6. *All the flip-chart sheets were displayed on the walls so that everyone could read them during the coffee-break.*

7. *Everybody gathered in the main room. They were randomly divided into subgroups of five each and were asked to discuss the points on the flip-chart sheets. After a while, we picked one person from each group to come together in front of the whole group and form a "reflecting team" who made comments about what they had been thinking. Then everybody returned to the subgroups and discussed what they had heard.*

This was another way to bring forth new feedback in the system and to put the participants into the observer position.

8. *The consultants discussed the process during the lunch break.*

From the feedback we had received, we found that the organization was very preoccupied with thoughts about pressure and ever-increasing demands from the outside. They wanted us to help them to cope with this pressure.

We followed the participants´ expectations by preparing some questions that focused on individual teacher's and the organization's possibilities for dealing with this pressure.

9. *The subgroups continued after lunch to work with these questions and to write their reflections on flip-chart sheets which everybody could read afterwards.*

10. *Finally, we re-formed the circle and made a "reflecting team" with a randomly selected group in the middle to get feedback.*

11. *The headmaster ended the day. He thanked the teachers for their participation and mentioned the possibility of a follow-up day. He thanked us as well.*

12. *We had a short meeting with the headmaster and the contact person, in which we made an evaluation.*

The headmaster was obviously relieved and thanked us for the day.

No previous arrangement for a follow-up consultation had been agreed, but the headmaster and the committee said that they would think it over.

In view of our experiences at the Danish seminars, we decided to offer the headmaster individual consultation. We wrote to him, but there was no response. So the consultation came to a halt at this point.

Reflections on dilemmas in the consultation

One of our dilemmas was that a small, but powerful, group of teachers was very eager to start the consultation by working towards definite goals, to make plans, and to change the organization, whereas we found it more helpful to start by understanding how things work in the organization. For example, how the suggestions about working with specific goals could be understood in the larger organizational context; what the consequences would be if we started by working with the goals, what it would mean to the other participants to work in that way; what dilemmas it would bring forth; and so on. We wanted to create a context in which all the participants would have the opportunity to think and talk about what they wanted to change and what they wanted to preserve in the organization and what their gains and losses might be.

In our original planning meeting, we had made it clear that we did not have the time both to clarify intentions, relations, and consequences of changes *and* to make specific plans. Therefore, we suggested that the consultation should be used to clarify intentions, relations, and consequences and that the consultees themselves could, afterwards, make specific plans for change (or for none) in the organization using this process.

Nobody opposed this suggestion, so we did not discuss it further, taking for granted that the lack of comments meant that the participants agreed. When we were subsequently supervised on the consultation, we recognized that some of the consultees may have been dissatisfied during the whole consultation, feeling that no final decisions had been made.

We have thought about the contradiction between our desire to focus on process and some of the teachers' efforts to work with plans for changing structure. Our implicit reason for focusing on processes is our hypothesis that the participants need a chance to share thoughts about changes and about consequences, without having any obligation to carry out these changes. Working too early towards specific ends might result in a situation in which the consultees keep their own wishes to themselves and cannot be open to others' ideas, because they are afraid of having to take responsibility for the consequences.

Had we been more attentive, we could have utilized the feedback by clarifying what this dilemma showed about the organization and about the relations between the energetic group of teachers, the other teachers, and the headmaster. However, we failed to focus on and uncover this contradiction.

Afterwards, we made a hypothesis that there was also a contradiction between some teachers who wanted an immediate change of the structure and others, including the headmaster, who feared focusing on specific changes because of fear of losing influence, control, or whatever.

The fact that we had only one day for consultation could be seen as connected with this contradiction. By limiting the consultation to one day the headmaster and the committee made sure that there was insufficient time to achieve fundamental changes; on the other hand, some of the other teachers became even more eager to make agreements on structural changes because they were afraid that nothing would change unless detailed long-term agreements were made during the consultation.

By missing the opportunity to clarify the dilemma of whether to focus on the process or to focus on making specific plans about change, we and the consultees missed an opportunity to recognize some important differences in the organization and the possibilities and restraints that these create for the members of the organization.

After the consultation, we formed another hypothesis: this dilemma could be a consequence of a contradiction between belief systems. It is as if we have one ideology and the consultees have another and that we had to convince them or to show them that our way of thinking and working in terms of focusing on process is the most useful for them. We even thought that if the consultees had had previous experience of process consultation, we would not have had the same trouble.

Process-oriented consultation is a helpful way to achieve insight into the relations in the organization, to clarify needs and desires, and to find new perspectives for change, whereas focusing too early on aims can result in insecurity and resistance. We take for granted that the consultees agree with us that insight is desirable, but we cannot be certain of this. Our idea about how change takes place might possibly be in conflict with the way of thinking in the organization.

How can we use this contradiction?

We wonder whether the organization necessarily has to accept our belief system to some degree, or whether it is sufficient if we as consultants make differences by intervening and creating feedback from our own point of view.

A guideline could be that our thinking and our way of putting questions and statements has to differ sufficiently from the consultees' way of thinking to make a difference. But if we, on the other hand, act too differently, it can be overwhelming for the consultees and there will be no change. So the question is whether our belief system differs too much from the belief system in the organization to make change happen or whether we can connect with the organization in some way that will reduce the differences and yet still make change possible.

DID WE SUCCEED?

Looking back at the various consultations we have done as rather inexperienced consultants, we have some doubts about our work and are not quite sure how to measure success in consultation.

We have seen all sorts of reactions after a consultation, from consultees applauding as a sign of satisfaction, to others who ignore our written request for feedback. Was the first reaction a sign of success as consultants and the latter a sign of failure?

Can we know at all whether the consultation is a success seen from the perspective of the organization, the staff, or the headmaster when we do not have a follow-up meeting or otherwise get feedback later on?

Certainly, we are used for several purposes by the various groups in an organization. In the consultation at the high school, we had the impression that the headmaster needed us to fail in order to confirm that improving management at the high school is impossible even though consultants are involved, and to show the staff that he has tried everything in order to improve relations at the school. At one of the first meetings, a teacher from the delegates' group even had a few words of warning for us. He told us that a year ago they had had a course in cooperation and that the instructor had been a failure and was laughed at by all the teachers. In other consultations, we have seen leaders trying to hand over leading responsibility that they themselves could not manage.

If our purpose is to help the organization to cope with troubles and if we succeed in doing this by being seen as "failures", are we then successful? If the organization is being relieved by transferring frustrations onto us as professionals who do not apparently offer any help and consequently chooses to solve the problems itself, have we then carried out our job? It might be said that we have succeeded in our purposes, but we doubt that we will succeed in

earning a living by doing consultation in this way! Or do we succeed only if all parties—the leader, the staff, and ourselves—are
satisfied with the outcome of the consultation?

It is our impression that this problem of getting a clear understanding of the extent to which a consultation has been successful
has been shared by the trainees at the Danish seminars.

We find consultation very exciting, but difficult. Some of our
troubles might be due to the jobs we have had and to our lack of
ability to define the tasks and to create a context with enough space
for constructive feedback.

Our own team of colleagues, which was established for the purpose of mutual help, was terminated when three of the five
members stopped doing consultations because they felt unappreci-
ated as consultants.

FURTHER REFLECTIONS

We are unsure whether we offered process consultation to the high
school without having clarified the contract sufficiently. Maybe we
were too eager to take the job, and maybe it is not always possible
to initiate change by process consultation. Possibly the organization
has to be prepared to work with process consultation to a certain
extent.

In retrospect we realize how hard it was to give suitable feedback on important signals from the consultees. Perhaps we should
have made use of even more reflections in front of or together with
the consultees to consider the process together.

We have also learned that we cannot just clarify the dilemmas in
the organization and afterwards make an ultimate plan.

There is a risk that we are organized by the hidden games in the
organization even though we try to take a meta-position and thus
avoid alliances.

CHAPTER 6

By which process do people learn to do consultation?

Berit Sander

T his is the story about my encounter with the systemic approach to consultation in groups and organizations. I shall try to draw a picture of the changes in my perception of problems, problem-solving, group processes, and ultimately in the way I picture the interacting world around me. It has been a very interesting personal development, but at the same time unexpectedly difficult and slow: you do not change your picture of the world overnight—not even over months. Why, then, should I want to work within the framework of this new concept? Let me try to explain.

GOOD-BYE, SCAPEGOATS

Analysing, describing, and recommending are all daily tools in the consultant's work when establishing change in organizations. Such tools are, of course, necessary and relevant for a structural kind of consultancy.

But the kind of consultancy work that addresses cooperation and management—that is, which is directly related to interrelations—

demands another approach. I will put it as strongly as to say that it is an explicit advantage to adopt a new "perception of the world" when our task is to be found within the context of relations and processes between people.

In the process of shifting focus from well-defined problems to relations, I have made an interesting observation. As an academic in this day and age, I am, as are all of us, so well schooled in the causal–logical way of thinking—the fact that we experience a world of cause and effect—that my brain gets close to developing an itch when I have to let go of this way of perception.

LIKE A NEW PICTURE OF THE WORLD

For several years I worked in an engineering company, which produces industrial pipe installations. I was in charge of personnel development and internal and external information activities. During that time, the idea of working as an external consultant took shape, and I started to prepare for this shift in occupation by attending a course in consultancy at a commercial college. Thus my path has led through traditional organizational theory and through traditional analysis and understanding of organizational problems.

As another supplement, and what I consider as a further development in my initially psychodynamic education from the university, I became interested in the systemic approach to organizational interventions. I heard about the Danish seminars when I was working at a consultancy company which was selling personal development courses to top managers. The consultants here were working very skilfully with individuals, but the ability to use group dynamics in the process were limited. I was interested in the shift of focus from individuals to group dynamics and processes between people. The systemic process-oriented way of consulting that I learned about at the Danish seminars gave me a picture of the world and a frame of understanding that brings me closer to the processes *inside* the organization—as a supplement to the basic, theoretical knowledge of organizational development, factors that limit and produce growth, the importance of structure, organization, and market relations, and so on.

The focus on processes has become even more relevant in my daily work, since I am now working as a consultant in a human resource consultancy company with very different tasks, all related to the development of organizations *through* the human resource perspective. A part of my job consists of recruiting personnel and managers, and that role is rather traditional consultancy work: analysing, describing, advising, and deciding. However, another part of my job consists of consultations to organizations or parts of organizations that want change in one way or another. And it has become very important to me to be able to shift my focus from either structure (and the like) or individuals to processes among individuals (i.e. group processes).

AN EXAMPLE

A group of social workers wants supervision. The group does not function well, the members are not able to support one another in their daily, demanding job performance, and there is a lot of stress and discomfort amongst them. Several of them are expressing both physical and psychological symptoms, such as stomach pains and temper tantrums, during their meetings. They all suffer from and complain about the very hostile atmosphere of these meetings.

I could choose to focus on the individual person, on his or her personal situation and specific characteristics. It would be possible for me to obtain certain information about each group member beforehand; for instance, it would be natural, as part of the remit of my company, to offer a personality test to the members in order to gain as much knowledge as possible about those involved. But I choose to focus on the processes in the group and between the members, and not on each person as an individual. I do not ask each member what his or her problem is; instead I ask the group to discuss why they want supervision right now, and not one year ago or in six months from now. I ask what changes the group wants and which signs might show that the change has occurred. I also ask what the group will lose when it does change.

While these questions are being discussed, I have the opportunity to focus on *the way* the participants relate to each other, looking for patterns and looking for the opposite: when the group describes itself as angry and internally disconnected, I ask them to describe what it is like when they are not. And I ask the group to reflect upon the consequences and the meaning to the group, and to their daily work, of the fact that different colleagues have different perspectives, ideas, experiences, and expectations. How can these differences be a weakness, and how can they be strengths?

In this way, I try to avoid focusing on the one or two persons who immediately are described as "The Problem". They might be, or they might not—I am not the one to contribute to the process of exclusion. My job is to clarify some patterns and to focus on some opportunities that the group, at this stage, does not itself see, and in this way provide some new energy to the system.

Using these systemic concepts has provided me with what I consider as an alteration to my picture of the world. I have found it useful to expand my perception of the world; at the same time, I have found it quite difficult. I have to get used to abandoning the wish of fully understanding a situation, a problem, an organization. As a traditional solver of problems, I am used to the straight and direct approach: a problem exists, I diagnose it, find a cure, and the result is recovery. When a fair amount of experience has been acquired, this "expert behaviour" gives the consultant a good deal of security: "I have seen this problem before, I know what it usually is about, and I have good empirical evidence of useful remedies." This approach gives me a feeling of quick perception of the case in hand, and I also have a relevant repertoire of possible "treatments".

SCAPEGOATS IN THE FRONT ROW

I have noticed that this way of approaching problems often leads to the naming of scapegoats. A problem and its interpretation is often related to "guilty" individuals. Then the solution to the problem is the removal of the individual. It might very well be true that a given cooperational problem relates to an individual. But it is much more interesting to see every individual as part of a relational context, and not—at least not in the first place—as good or bad persons *as such*. The consultant must be able to work in this relational field where the focal point shifts from the individual to the group's interaction. In this way I, as a consultant, contemplate *relations* between persons and activities which produce and maintain a given relation, with much less emphasis on the characteristics of the individual.

I think this is a very important point: when working in the field of cooperation we cannot continually maintain a belief in the removal of the diagnosed problem-holder as the main cure. Whom do we blame next?

AN EXAMPLE

At a team-building seminar for a managerial group whose place of work was undergoing a major expansion—including an imminent merger—the group emphasized the necessity of cooperation in order to deal with the future demands of organizational development while at the same time maintaining intensive and complicated production levels.

It was agreed that the cooperation would imply a great deal of openness. The group perceived and described itself as well functioning and open, but at a certain point I sensed very different individual perceptions of the managerial group's real openness and, as a consequence, of its real cooperation. In order to visualize these different perceptions of what seemed to be the same situation, I asked each manager to describe his own degree of openness to and willingness for dialogue as compared to the rest of the group. The first time around this process was not very useful, because each of them—precisely as a consequence of the lack of openness—avoided any differentiation between colleagues, fearing to expose any one of them or himself. So the exercise did not *in itself* produce any new information for the group. But something interesting happened when two managers clashed with mutual accusations of how the other made it impossible to cooperate and practise openness. This gave me an opportunity to point out—in the actual situation—what was going on *here and now* by giving direct feedback. I asked the two persons involved to explain what they each had heard the other one say, and what in the other's attitude resulted in this conclusion. And then they each had the opportunity to explain what the intention was, which obviously was received differently by the other, and vice versa. By focusing on the way the two colleagues communicated, it became clear to them and to the rest of the group that the problem lay in the way they communicated and not in their intentions.

By focusing on the process as such—*how* the two colleagues communicated—everybody realized that the "unfeeling" colleague was not to blame for the poor cooperation and the below-zero dialogue. The mistrustful and rejecting mode of contact was maintained in the process of communication. Simultaneously, it became generally obvious that the solution to the problem was not to be found in a "change" or removal of the "unfeeling" colleague, but in a change in the relational framework of the two colleagues, by providing knowledge and feedback about underlying expectations and intentions. In that instant the scapegoat of the managerial group, the "unfeeling" colleague, disappeared and the problem became the mode of communication and the lack of feedback.

A GOOD QUESTION

To avoid the tendency towards the naming of scapegoats, while trying to see some patterns in a problematic or unfruitful teamwork, I must stay in a detached position: not choosing sides and not perceiving the interrelational processes as noise on the line but as "*the* highway" to information and feedback—and thus to change and development. My aim is to *create the framework for a process* instead of *controlling the content* (in order to get to the "heart of the matter"). Thereby I abandon the role as the visible and controlling analyst who must always be a jump ahead, trying to provide explanations and answers. By contrast, I pose questions to reveal the main actors' own versions and own knowledge. For example, I explore differences: "When your colleague spoke, did you then hear something different from what you expected?", or "What was most different in the group's discussion?", not "What was right?" or "Did you agree?" My questions are meant to focus on differences. When exploring differences, the focus is on movement. This creates visibility, which I consider an important first step towards development and change. A metaphor from a different world comes to mind: dogs can only catch sight of objects that are moving, even though they usually have excellent eyesight. When you throw a toy, the dog is able to catch it in the air, even in the twilight. But as soon as the object has landed and is lying still on the ground, the dog finds it very difficult to catch sight of it to continue the play. The dog runs around in bigger and bigger circles, to and fro, with its nose to the ground until it finally finds the object, probably with the aid of its excellent sense of smell.

Movements are essential to activate the dog's excellent eyesight. In the case of stagnation, the dog acts like a short-sighted person searching by hand for spectacles lying on the table just in front of him or her, not being able to see what is right there.

To be able to act—for instance, to create changes and development—you have to establish visibility. (If you can't see it, you can't do anything about it.) To create visibility you have to establish motion, or else you cannot catch sight of it, just like the dog. I might call this phenomenon "The Dog's Sight", and it reminds me to go for the differences in order to create motion, visibility, and finally the ability to act.

The focus on differences is established with the aid of posing questions that explore differences.

AN EXAMPLE

The marketing manager of a manufacturing company described how he never received any feedback or reactions to his initiatives. He had just terminated a demanding and extensive task and had no idea of how the other managers felt about his effort and whether they appreciated it. I asked: "How is this different from the rest in the executive group?" He answered that it was the same for the others. I asked: "Does that mean that you, in the executive group, never respond to one another? That nobody ever knows if others think that you have done a good job?" He answered this question affirmatively, with surprise spreading over his face. It dawned on him that his position was not special—that is, it did not necessarily have anything to do with him personally but, rather, was the result of the way the group habitually related to one another, and was obviously similar for all the executive group. He had never regarded the matter in this light before, and he looked relieved.

Asking a group the appropriate questions places energy and focus inside the group, rather than being drawn from within the consultant. By asking instead of answering, we find the experts among the consultees and not among the consultants. The focal point becomes the relations of the group—where the insight is—and the energy of the group is mobilized. It is here that the real work potential lies; and from here the group will remain active when the consultant has left.

THE CONSULTANT'S GAINS AND LOSSES

It seems that the systemic way of working with consultancy introduces a dilemma in the traditional perception of the consultant and his or her role as agent of change. The consultant's position and visible control and power change and so too does the immediate perception—also self-perception—of the consultant as "The Person in Charge".

Learning to take the systemic "consultant position" is, as mentioned earlier, to a very large degree a case of absorbing an altered picture of the world. At the same time, of course, we need some concrete techniques—for example, questioning methods, ways of forming hypotheses—that support our position as agents of change and process consultants. These can be presented on courses or in books, but techniques and methods do not, in effect, become meaningful until we put them into practice. Learning systemic process consulting is learning by doing, *par excellence*.

We can learn some techniques and methods in advance, but it all boils down to assuming a consulting position in the group that summoned us as agents of change. And this requires a special kind of personal daring and a willingness to run risks, as we have placed ourselves in an unpredictable, uncontrolled field—in a web of relations and several assorted versions of a reality we seemingly share.

When the consultancy role is thus described, we must possess a peculiar mixture of dominance and reservedness, a difficult mixture of waiting and guiding: an ability to be a "non"-person, abandoning personal safety and control of the situation when, at the same time, the client strongly demands our visibility and willingness to act. We have to trust our own perceptions even when they are in conflict with the traditional demands for a successful consultation. We must be able to keep quiet and let the process run—often for much longer than might be expected from a traditional consultant with the supposed amount of immediate power of action, suggestions for solutions, and plans of action. As a systemic-based process consultant, I float in a room of not-understanding and multiple versions, with no unequivocal answers to look for. I have to listen to what is happening, form my hypotheses, and ask my questions in order to mobilize the participants' own knowledge. Using my questions, I work with clarifications rather than provide interpretations. I try continually to stay in the process by asking questions—and not establishing explanations and answers. And one of the dilemmas of this consulting position is perhaps that I miss the high of interpretation: miss not being the one who brings forth the conclusions and enjoys the role of the one who grasps the overall picture, sees the patterns, and understands the meaning— but "just" being the one who poses the questions.

The role dilemma: do I lose control?

A process consultant works much more with clarifications and implications than with causes and effects. This is the real difference when we begin working with systemic consultation. But the instant I stop finding and describing "The Truth"—the correct configuration, version, diagnosis, and so on—the firm ground slips from under my consultant's feet. Not having an unequivocal version of the truth, I do not have an unequivocal explanation. And in this way I lose a relatively easy access to the potentially "right" solution to offer my client. The solution becomes inherent in the process. And I, the consultant, must be able to float in a space of not-understanding. I must be able to accept the problems without immediately describing, understanding, and treating them. As a consultant I shall have to give up understanding what the problem "really" is and instead create room for change by posing questions that bring differences into focus, thereby creating new perspectives to a given dilemma, situation, version.

It is a mental challenge to abandon an unequivocal understanding of the organization and its problems, bearing in mind that I use my understanding of a given situation to gain control over it, which again gives me a feeling of professional and personal security. Giving up control is the same thing as inviting unpredictability and insecurity. Thus, in the process of learning the systemic perception of the world, the most important thing for me has been the "aha!" experience of discovering that I am in fact able to be in this space of not-understanding and—as a consequence—of no-control: enduring the problems without immediately finding "The Cure".

The role dilemma: do I lose power and influence?

Working with questions instead of answers—or, say, with process instead of content—puts the consultant in a role dilemma. The expert role, with its competence, power, and prestige, is distinctly more visible and in line with our traditional views on successful behaviour. Is it sufficiently fun and rewarding to be the Questioner and not the one who has the answers? Do I feel enough "in charge"? I must be attracted both to the role of being visible and powerful and to the potential influence in order to seek the role as consultant in the first place. When I then enter the domain of cooperation I must abandon—at least on and off—these very same characteristics, and for long stretches assume a reflective attitude. I realize that handling these shifting roles demands a high degree of awareness and flexibility.

A DIFFERENT FOCUS
THAT MAKES A DIFFERENCE

AN EXAMPLE

I was discussing a project with a colleague, an experienced human resource consultant. We were planning a process for a managerial group in a private company producing software solutions. My colleague wanted to start the project by interviewing each manager about his personal history, his values, his motivational factors, his strengths and weaknesses, his evaluation of the other managers' strengths and weaknesses, and so on. I was more interested in the interpersonal relations and the different views of the group's strengths and weaknesses, what kind of change the group expected, how changes would show, the gains and losses connected to a given change, and so on. We discussed

these very different focuses and I mentioned that his individual-
ized approach would bring into focus an evaluation of the individual manager, inevitably pointing out who was strong and
who was weak or even unqualified. I did not consider this as a
part of the task as put to us by the executive manager.

My colleague pointed out to me that if I stuck to the idea of
not approaching the group *through* the individual manager, I was
challenging the basic concept of the company in which we were
employed. Did I *really* want that? And, as I understood was being asked between the lines, was I, by introducing a focus that
was very different from the traditional one, really a part of the
team? I thus became aware of another type of dilemma in my
personal process of learning a different approach to consultation.

It is difficult to learn the mental shift from focusing on the problem—for instance, an unsuccessful manager—and its exact solution
to dealing with the process surrounding the problem: the implications of the problem, its significance to the individual and the
organization, the advantages and drawbacks of its existence and—
also—of its disappearance. Instead of understanding the problem
in a field of cause and effect, I have to contribute to a process in
which the participants get to communicate their individual version
of reality: how the situation looks from the individual point of view
as opposed to the colleague's version of the exact same situation. In
the nature of the matter there can never really be an "exact same
situation". The number of versions equals the number of individuals, a fact that poses quite a challenge to the consultant working
with the description and understanding of problems as a starting
point. Which understanding are we to use, and which one is
wrong? This line of thought is no longer valid once we have realized the extent to which the world is built upon an infinite number
of perceptions of reality.

THE QUALITY OF ACTIONS

How can I, as a consultant, carry such a process through? Initially,
it is important that I am conscious of my own role as a "neutral"
person who does not seek to reveal "the real truth" but whose task
is to create room for the individual to become aware of, and make

visible, his version of reality. The greater the knowledge of, and feedback on, the different versions of reality, the broader the common picture upon which action is possible. During the process preceding decisions, the work to establish a common picture (arising from the many versions of reality) is necessary in order to secure the quality of the decisions and actions and the later loyalty to the changes. Otherwise we are left paralyzed, unable to decide which description of the situation is to form a basis for the necessary actions. This common picture is created through communication.

Now things are getting really complicated! After pinpointing that there is no one right version of reality, but as many versions as there are participants in a given context, I say that, in the end, we need a uniform picture of a given situation after all. My point is that staying in the process of elaborating on the many versions of a given situation gives a lot of feedback about the situation. The involved parties are heard, their points of views are respected, different information is put forward by them, which establishes a broader fundament to act upon when action becomes necessary. Constantly, situations in the daily life of cooperation require concrete problem-solving: that is, decision-making. And when we reach the point of making decisions we have to transform the multiversion picture of the problem to a more unambiguous one. In the end we might decide to fire the unsuccessful manager, concluding that he actually is the biggest part of the problem.

CHANGES WITHIN REACH

It feels as though the brain has to be turned in a new direction to think beyond causal logic. And why is that desirable, being so troublesome? Apart from the difficulties, systemic thinking is so loaded with "aha!" experiences that establishing a concept of the world based upon it is mental joy. From a consultant's point of view, it opens a world of possible developments when focus shifts from problems, individual faults, and the incompetence of groups caused by individual errors and shortcomings. It seems to me to be far more constructive, and in the realm of the realistic, to reach for change by acting upon the interpersonal relations—thus influencing the perception of a given situation and, as a result, the corresponding behaviour—instead of trying to change individuals through individually aimed interventions. That kind of activity—more like therapy—is not the tool for me as an organizational consultant. My efforts would drown in the complicated sea of relations in groups and organizations. It wouldn't show a ripple on the water, and bearing in mind the motive for people, or at least for me, to become an organizational consultant—the wish to influence—even a visible ripple wouldn't always be enough. Sometimes you wish for a wave to follow you—to make a difference.

CHAPTER 7

Converting a teaching event into consultation

Jan Fjordbak

INTRODUCTION: BACKGROUND AND AIM

T his chapter is about learning the important skills that you have to develop before starting out to do consultation, about reorganizing your previous and on-going experiences to become part of a consultant's identity, and about creating small-scale opportunities to practice consultation.

In recent years, we have seen an increasing interest in consultation work in a broader sense. The number of consultants has increased, and professionals occupied in other functions are trying to work in a more consultative way. In Denmark, this tendency is very visible in areas like school counselling and public agencies supporting developmental activities in the social services, unemployment, the occupational health service, and so forth. It seems as though everybody wants to be a consultants nowadays. Nobody wants to do the real work any more: being a consultant to people doing real work carries more prestige—even better, being a consultant to consultants!

The people who are becoming interested in systemic consultation are mostly social workers with a background in family counselling and psychologists with a clinical background. Some are pressured by their employers, others are themselves eager to expand their field of working into consultation.

Some people with a background in consultation do, of course, become interested in systemic thinking, but the majority of participants in systemic consultation courses have their background in the field of family therapy and move from that position towards consultation. Because of the lack of consultation work experiences, training is much needed.

My background was neither family therapy nor consultation work. I was rather new to both fields. I was engaged in my training as an organizational psychologist and completing a thesis on systemic consultation. At the same time, I earned my living working as a child-care worker in a day-care institution for mentally retarded children. I wished to expand my area of functioning from child-care work to consultation. I was looking out for any opportunity to pick up teaching or consultation challenges; this chapter describes the outcome of one such opportunity.

From my own experience, the key issues in getting started are the following:

- How can you establish opportunities to practice consultation in your own organization?
- What do you have to consider before starting a consultation?
- What do you have to consider during the consultation?
- What do you have to give up in order to do consultation?

THE SKILLS OF CONSULTATION

Before I try to describe my own learning process, I would like to offer my ideas about the required skills for doing consultation.

As a systemic consultant you need to master what I call *general consultant skills* to be able to negotiate contracts with your clients. This requires knowledge about organizational processes as well as general communication skills. These skills are needed to be able to ensure a sufficient uncovering of the problem and a mutual clarification of the purpose of the consultation.

In addition, the consultant needs to be able to *design* a consultation that will facilitate changes. [This is where consultation methods differ from each other. Some will be based on first-order cybernetics, where the system is observed and analysed by an outsider. Inadequate or insufficient patterns of interaction are revealed, good or vicious circles are identified. Interventions aim towards reflection and insight in these patterns, and towards the creation of new patterns of interaction. Other methods will be based on second-order cybernetics, in which the idea is to use the consultant–client interaction to create space for reflection and experimentation with new actions. This approach emphasizes the process and views the consultant as a part of this process instead of seeing the consultant as an expert, who must lead the consultation in a specific direction.] This again requires a good deal of insight into human and organizational processes combined with a *theory of change* based upon the fundamental assumptions of systemic thinking.

Furthermore, you need to know how to use yourself as a tool in a process of change. You also need to master some *techniques* to get these processes going. You need to have a repertoire from which to pick your interventions.

METHODS TO ACQUIRE
THE NECESSARY QUALIFICATIONS

The issue of learning consultation can now be phrased as a question of getting access to opportunities to acquire and train in the above-mentioned skills. There is no single answer to this question but a multiplicity of possibilities, and one must use as many of them as possible:

- literature about systemic thinking
- courses to build knowledge and train general consultant skills (for instance, through role play and exercises)
- trying to incorporate systemic ideas and methods into your day-to-day work
- writing down experiences
- receiving supervision

These opportunities are all well known, but I will add to this list an approach that I have used to great advantage. It is the possibility of creating small-scale "consultancy-like" events at your own place of work (or in organizations to which you are connected through your job). The idea is to use existing contacts to create opportunities to practise consultation.

The rest of this chapter deals with one such "consultation-like" event, which I conducted at my workplace in 1993. I will focus on my reflections before, during, and after the event and end by extracting some general learning points.

SELF-INITIATED MINI-CONSULTATION
AS A LEARNING PROCESS

The mini-consultation I describe took place between the first and second of the Danish seminars. The event was a three-hour course about burnout at my workplace, which was a day-care institution for mentally retarded children. At the time there were ten employees working in three groups.

The whole thing started as a loose idea during a large planning seminar in the institution. Someone wanted to know more about the burnout syndrome, a subject that I had briefly introduced earlier. I therefore offered to arrange a three-hour course, seeing an opportunity to try out some of my new learning about systemic methods.

At the outset, my role was to teach my colleagues about burnout. However, I saw this as a chance not only to pass on some information, but also to create space for reflection about some important issues concerning the conditions of work. Perhaps I could start some developmental processes in the organization. The idea was to drag in some elements of consultation and make the course an intervention pushing forward organizational development. I tried to think about my role from a consultant's point of view, so the weight was put on the actual needs of the organization rather than optimizing the transference of knowledge about the burnout phenomenon.

At a staff meeting, I asked people to clarify what they wanted from the course. There was a general wish for a combination of an introduction and exercises, but apart from that I was given a relatively free hand to design the event as I desired. In terms of contracting this was not very explicit (there was no formal contract), but I felt that we had formed a psychological contract that was sufficiently clear to go on.

Summarizing, I grabbed at the wish for information and dragged it in the direction of consultation. The idea of having a course was not mine, but the consultation element was; in this sense, I call the consultation self-initiated.

The programme for the course was designed in the following way:

1. *Introduction, with discussion* about the burnout syndrome and how it is related to other stress reactions. The basic concepts I expounded upon were Christina Maslach's (1982) three dimensions of burnout: emotional exhaustion (feeling used up), depersonalization (distancing and development of negative attitudes towards clients, etc.), and personal accomplishment (reduced self-esteem, feeling of personal defeat). These were used to separate the state of burnout from related phenomena such as psychological tiredness, stress, depression, and crisis. Then I introduced the theory of coping as developed by the Lazarus group (cf. Lazarus & Folkman, 1984). In the light of this concept, burnout can be seen as the result of exaggerated use of inadequate coping strategies like distancing, self-control, escape, and avoidance (Rasmussen, 1990).

2. *Mutual interview in pairs*, with an interview guide focusing on each person's own experiences and ways of coping with stressful situations. The questions were inspired by the theory of coping and by solution-focused therapy, putting emphasis on resources and actual behaviour. One such question was: "What are you doing now to prevent yourself from burning out?" The pairs were formed as a means to create new relations between persons who usually did not work closely together—in other words, to create new feedback.

3. *Feedback* from the exercise, with focus on what each person had learned.

4. *Introduction with discussion* about how to prevent and reduce

burnout, including an introduction to different levels of intervention. The levels were individual, interpersonal, work unit,
and organizational, and on each level the interventions could
aim at identification, prevention, adaptation, or rehabilitation
(cf. Jenner & Segraeus, 1989).

5. *Sequential discussions,* addressing in what sense burnout was a
current problem in the institution and what to do about it.

6. *Planning of initiatives*—actual planning of actions to prevent
burnout at the institution. This included establishing which
people were to be responsible for carrying out the decisions.

The actual content of the different steps is described in more detail
below.

The systemic elements were to be found primarily in the mutual
interviews and the sequential discussion, in which I put the systemic assumptions and the systemic techniques into practice. I
regard the mutual interviews primarily as an intervention of first-
order systemic thinking, the creation of new feedback in the
organization, while I see the sequential discussion as a second-order
intervention—the creation of room for negotiation of a new reality, a
sort of organizational self-reflection. The planning section was also a
distinct consultative element, although not specifically systemic.

I now describe the considerations I went through before, during,
and after the mini-consultation.

Can you do consultation to your own colleagues?

The first worry I had to deal with was the question of doing consultation to my own colleagues. Would I be able to be objective
enough? Would I be recognized in the position? And how would
things work out? Would a professional, experienced consultant say
yes to a task like this?

Despite these fears, I decided to go through with the consultation
and tried to reframe my worries into questions of how to do it.

I was aware that I needed to pay specific attention to the dilemma of being part of the group and, at the same time, standing
outside of it. To some extent this is the key issue for any internal
consultant. And in this respect I found the systemic framework

helpful in pointing out two aspects as critical: firstly, the issue of obtaining and staying in a sufficiently neutral position; secondly, the issue of getting permission to and being able to assume an observing (meta) position.

The observer position

I chose to present my introduction about burnout as a means of passing on knowledge from some books I had read. I was afraid of putting myself in a one-up position as an expert on my colleagues' work, so I decided not to present my view of burnout as "The expert analysis, ex cathedra". I presented Christina Maslach's view of burnout because I found it easy to comprehend, and I emphasized that it was one out of many possible views of burnout. I deliberately avoided a presentation of a systemic view of burnout (cf. Fruggeri & McNamee 1991), because I was afraid that it would be too advanced. [In Fruggeri & McNamee, 1991, burnout is perceived in a second-order systemic view, in accordance with the idea that "the problem creates a system". The authors point to the fact that many of the steps traditionally recommended to prevent burnout (i.e. reduced involvement) are actually part of the syndrome itself: thinking of yourself as burned-out creates a system of behaviour that will maintain the problem.]

On the other hand, I did some serious arguing with myself about this, because it was not a very systemic way of starting out. In a second-order view it would be problematic to deliver too many definitions. It is more the process by which the organization makes its own definitions that is of interest. As a way of exploring this issue, I would have liked to start out with a more open-ended discussion without the initial theoretical input, but I actually thought that this would have made me seem too distant or too intangible, as a person asking too many questions and coming up with no answers. Flip-chart presentation was well known and safe, so I stuck to that.

I thought that taking the observer position right from the start was too much of a challenge. I was too unsure as to whether I would be allowed to take this meta-position and leaned towards the more well-known role of the teacher with a "down-to-earth" message.

Another example of trying to keep my role clear was during the pairs exercise at the beginning of the event. I might, as an external consultant, have wandered around listening to the conversations, but as an internal consultant I thought this would be getting too close. It would have underlined my special position too much, or I might have been seen as an intruder. Perhaps this was a consequence of redefining the context from teaching to consultation: in teaching settings, with greater distance between the participants and the subject, the teacher will be more welcome to inspect the exercises than will the consultant in a consultation in which there are "real personal problems" at stake.

The feedback from the exercise was led by me. I asked questions about their learning, and the answers were mostly directed at me. I just listened, trying to stay in a meta-position. In general people were not burned out, but maybe sometimes stressed. They found it helpful to share these experiences. One person said that during the exercise she had become aware that she was relying too heavily on inadequate coping strategies like denial and self-control.

During the sequential discussion my intentions were solely to guide the process. I presented the task, which was to reflect upon how and to what extent burnout was a problem at the institution. This was purposely a very open instruction and created some insecurity. The head of the unit therefore encouraged me to take the lead and make the first reflection, and I consented. In this way I was not permitted to stay outside the group in this exercise; instead, I had a dual position as both participant and leader of the process. This felt difficult, but I started with a general statement: in my view, the institution had a great advantage in preventing burnout because of the fact that the children were only there for about two-and-a-half hours every day, a relatively short time in which you could hardly get very stressed. The next person then took up this idea but turned it upside down. She stated that because of the very short time they had with the children, it was very difficult to do a good job. This again led to some of the next speakers wondering about high levels of ambition as a critical factor in burnout.

In the exercise there was insufficient time for many considerations about my dual role, but in retrospect this dual role may not have been such a bad solution after all. By taking the lead and contributing with my hypothesis, I was surely influencing the content of the exercise but in a context where my viewpoint was only to be taken as one out of many possible viewpoints.

What happened here by coincidence might be of more general interest, as a way of coping with the internal consultant's primary dilemma: simultaneously being part of the group and taking a meta-position. The dilemma is temporarily resolved by inviting the whole group to join the consultant in taking the meta-position. The participants are invited to step outside their organization and, from that viewpoint, produce hypotheses about it. Thereby, they are getting closer to the role of the consultant. And when the internal consultant takes an active part in the exercise, he similarly is getting closer to the role of the participants. In this way the systemic idea of facilitating change by helping the members of an organization to look at themselves from an observer position helps the internal consultant to cope with the insider–outsider dilemma.

Neutrality

The second part of the sequential discussion resulted in a lot of suggestions about what the organization could do to prevent burn-out. Some wanted more honesty in communication, some more feedback, some reallocation of tasks—clarification of areas of responsibility. There were also suggestions about social activities, like going to the cinema together and so forth. The suggestions were put on a flip chart, and I led the discussion about implementation.

As an internal consultant, it is always a difficult challenge to lead discussions amongst your colleagues about implementation. You are putting yourself in a position close to that of manager, which could be provocative in several ways. As an internal consultant it becomes crucial how your position in the group is already viewed and how good you are at keeping a neutral position. If you are not respected and do not have the confidence of your colleagues, you should not try internal consultancy at all. But even when you have their respect, it is very important to behave in such a way that you maintain this atmosphere of mutual respect and confidence at all times. In this case I felt pretty sure about having their respect and confidence, and I did not predict any difficulties.

The event proceeded smoothly most of the way, until the suggestion about going to the cinema came up. I did not agree with that and started to argue against it. The suggestion was then turned down, as a common decision, but left open for individual initiative. My negative attitude towards this suggestion created some discomfort. I can now see what happened: it was a mistake to interfere with the content of this decision. I reacted spontaneously having in mind an earlier experience of going to the cinema together, which I had disliked. But with hindsight I think that my reaction also had something to do with my relationship with the proposer. In some respects I had a competitive relationship with this person, which made me react negatively. Anyway, temporarily I had dropped out of the consultant role.

From this I learned how important it is to stay neutral. An internal consultant must renounce influencing the content of the decisions the consultation might end up with. It will be regarded as a violation of trust if you use your position as process leader to force your own points of view through. You must leave the leading of the decision-making parts of the consultation to the manager, If you cannot let go of directly influencing the content of decisions, you should give up the whole idea of doing internal consultation. Giving up influence on content is the price to pay for being given the privilege of leading the process.

I have also learned to be very conscious about my relationships to the different individuals I consult, trying for myself to redefine the relationship (i.e. from a competitive to a respectful, helping relationship) before starting the consultation.

This little intermezzo was, fortunately, only a minor detail, one that did not ruin the general experience of a good and constructive process. There were even visible results: a rather diffuse wish for preventing burnout was transformed into a decision about improving possibilities for mutual feedback by organizing a course with this purpose. People were made responsible for working with the clarification of the allocation of tasks—and we all had a very amusing evening at the cinema!.

The feedback

First of all, I see the enthusiasm and the amount and quality of reflections during the course as important feedback, telling me that I was doing all right.

In the evaluation the participants said that it had been exciting and inspiring to try new ways of talking about their work. The interviews and the sequential discussions were especially commended. The participants would have liked more time for interviews, my handwriting was criticized, and they missed having photocopies of the introduction to make it easier to follow. I took this in immediately, but I also see it as a sign that the theoretical presentation was too comprehensive. From this I have learned not to take too much time performing as a teacher. I must also keep in mind that my own need to be the centre of attention should not overshadow the needs of the group. The theoretical presentation was too much an attempt to "transfer information" and too little the creation of common understanding. In future, I will put more weight on dialogue and mutual exploration of the conceptualization process itself. There were many questions about how to distinguish between burnout and the related phenomena with private ethology. This could have been used for a shared exploration.

What made things happen were the exercises in which the systemic theories of change were implemented. This supported my belief in systemic exercises as useful tools in the consultation process.

The feedback that pleased me the most was hearing later that the head of the unit had recommended me to her colleagues. This strengthened my self-confidence as a consultant. I felt supported in my role as consultant, which encouraged me to continue.

In terms of evaluation of effect, it is very difficult to say whether a given result is caused by a specific event or not, especially when you are dealing with a complex phenomenon like burnout. However, following this event, the staff were interested in discussing ways to introduce supervision as a tool for developing the organization and as a key tool in preventing burnout. Supervision has subsequently been implemented in terms of a course in collegial (peer) supervision, which I have now conducted over a period of nine months. It would appear that the supervision is about to become an integral part of the work, which means that the organization now has a built-in remedy for preventing burnout.

The burnout course also formed a base for other, more "pure" consultation tasks, which were offered to me, first, as an internal consultant on cooperational difficulties and leader of planning seminars and, later, via recommendations for consultancy and supervision in other systems. So this event became an important building brick in my experience and career.

GENERAL LEARNING POINTS

Becoming a skilled systemic consultant depends on trying it out and learning from your successes and mistakes—that is, learning by doing.

In this cumbersome process of gathering experience, I have found it useful to drag tasks originally formulated as teaching tasks into consultancy, with a positive outcome for all the participants involved. The organization gets the benefit of an intervention specifically directed towards its needs, and the possibility of ending up with decisions about new actions; the consultant gets useful experience in working with systemic methods. You can thus base your safety on the more well-known teaching role and from here move into the more insecure pioneering role of a process-oriented consultant. When you succeed in this you have the possibility of getting feedback that can help you form and strengthen your identity as a consultant. The feeling of being successful makes it easier to be open to criticism and suggestions for improvements.

In spite of the difficulties involved, I would recommend anyone learning consultation to pick up potential consultancy tasks within their own place of work. But be sure to think through your consultant role thoroughly: with yourself (self-reflection), with someone from outside the organization (a supervisor), and with the involved participants (negotiation of contract). It is also important that, if you are responsible for the process, you can and do give up the intention of directly influencing the content of decisions. As internal consultant you must concentrate upon leading the process, leaving the content of decisions to be decided by the group only. This can be very difficult when the decisions relate to your own working conditions as well. It is here that concepts like neutrality and the observer position can be very helpful. The closer you are to the people you will be a consultant to, the more attention you must pay to these issues.

CHAPTER 8

A story of unheeded warning lights and a semi-external consultant

Bodil Pedersen

T his is a story about some obvious and simple "mistakes" and their consequences.

It is also a story about failure to pay attention to one's own warning lights because of being in too much of a hurry and wanting to take shortcuts. What often happens then is that one loses direction.

SOME HISTORY

I was asked to give a "course" for a community psychological counselling service, which has its office in a community centre. The clients are people of a wide range of ages and from varied social backgrounds. The counselling service offers 10 one-hour sessions of therapy and is free of charge. Therapy is mainly conducted as individual therapy. The counselling service has existed since the mid-1970s and was originally organized as a day unit. A couple of years ago an evening unit was started up.

The members of the staff are psychology students and newly graduated psychologists. There has been some turnover in the staff group, and a little over one-third of the staff members of the whole counselling service are new. As a supervisor I, like the counsellors themselves, offered my services free of charge. The fact that everybody including the supervisor was doing volunteer work, and had specifically chosen to work with this counselling service, created a special and personal bond between the people involved.

The day group and the evening group work separately, each with its own supervisor, but they constitute one economic unit and to a certain degree a single operational unit, having monthly common meetings.

I am a psychologist, and at the time of the request I had been supervisor to the evening unit for approximately one year. I met fortnightly with the group for two hours of supervision of the therapy sessions that the counsellors had conducted that same evening. The therapy sessions chosen for supervision were selected by the counsellors themselves according to their needs. The supervision consisted in the counsellors who had conducted the selected therapy session being interviewed by one of the other counsellors, with the rest of the counsellors and I serving as a reflecting team.

The evening unit suggested that I should run this course, and the request was presented to me through one of its members. The request was to spend two days working with the topics "How to use the resources of the counselling group optimally", and/or "Women counselling women", and/or "How to spot and support the resources of the clients".

There was some initial muddle about the contents of the request, that is, the priority given to each of the proposed themes, and whether the service wished to work with all of them or would accept picking out one. The request had apparently been agreed on at the common meeting of the two groups. It was only after several telephone calls between myself and the contact person that the contents were finally settled.

I had, for reasons of time, refused to work with all the suggested themes. According to the contact person, the theme of the course was, then, to be "How to use the resources of the counselling service optimally", and the participants of the course wanted it to be based on exercises related to their own practice, rather than primarily on lectures.

The only information I received on the background for the request was that the counselling service had received some money for courses from a fund, that the evening group had put forward my name for running the course, and that the day unit had thought it was a good idea because I had personal experience with the kind of work they were doing. The course started more than four months after the request had originally been made.

When I first received the request, I saw it as a good opportunity to follow up my own learning process at the Danish seminars in systemic consultation which I was attending at the time. Subsequently, however, a lot of pressure accumulated, both at work and in my private life, to an extent that made me wish that I had not accepted the job. At this point, warning lights were blinking somewhere on the periphery of my mind, but I paid little attention to them at the time. I shall return later in this article to these warning lights and my reasons for not heeding them.

PLANNING FOR THE COURSE

Since I was attending a course in systemic consultation, there were a number of concepts, questions, and working methods I had been presented with that I was eager to explore in my work with the group(s):

1. *The reasons for the contents of the request, and why it had been made at that specific time:* exploring this issue can imply that the consultant obtains information about the history of the development of the organization, about how the request came about, about the structure of the system, and about the positions and functions of its individual members. This means acquiring knowledge about formal and informal structures and about what these structures mean to the individuals involved. This helps the consultant to make a hypothesis about the actual dynamics of a system and about why someone sees a need for consultation.

2. *The concept of feedback:* to be able to manage productive change, a system needs internal and external feedback. If a system, or part

of a system, does not get the necessary feedback, it has a tendency to get stuck—that is, to become less productive.

Feedback is the response that the system, the subsystem, or
the individual receives at any given time. Internal feedback is
feedback within the system; external feedback is feedback from
the environment in which the system operates.

To help a system change, a consultant may, in the course of a
consultation, facilitate internal feedback and thereby improve
the system's general awareness about itself. To help the system
maintain the advantages of this newly acquired feedback, it is
helpful to explore, and thereby increase, awareness of how the
system gets external and internal feedback. It is also helpful to
make it possible for the system to develop ways of ensuring
feedback in the future.

The way feedback works is, among others, that it makes
productive changes in beliefs possible→changes in beliefs again
make way for changes in behaviour→changes in behaviour
create possibilities for developing new relationships in which
beliefs again may develop→and so on.

3. *The question of group members feeling disconnected:* if feedback
   loops cease to function, there is a great risk that individuals in
   the system will feel disconnected from the system as a whole,
   which again will hamper the flow of feedback, thus increasing
   the risk of individuals getting disconnected and weakening the
   possibilities of the system adapting to new challenges and needs,
   and so forth.

4. *The concepts of gains and losses in the process of change:* when a
   system gets stuck, it becomes inflexible, stops changing, and
   therefore becomes unable to meet the needs in a world of changing systems and individuals with changing needs. When this
   happens, very often some individuals within a system will perceive the need for doing things differently, the need for change.
   By changing the ways of doing things, dilemmas may be solved
   and gains obtained, but advantages of doing things the old way
   may be lost.

   One of the losses is often that there might be a threat to the
   sense of security that doing things the way "they have always

been done" has given. Some individuals within the system might be more concerned than others about the losses.

I felt somewhat unsure of what plans to make for the course, mainly because I had received the request, mainly over the phone, from one person only, who additionally was from the subgroup I knew. I had no first-hand knowledge of the day unit whatsoever, and I had not had the opportunity to negotiate the contract with the whole counselling group or at least with representatives from both subgroups. Neither had I had occasion to discuss with the group why they had formulated this request at this specific time, nor to interview the group about their organization.

As a result, I had little information to help me make and test the hypothesis on which I was going to base the plan for carrying out the course.

To get inspiration I therefore turned to my notes from the Danish seminars, which I was then attending. At this course, I had been presented with the idea that dilemmas that were in the way of change were often caused by lack of feedback in the system, by lack of knowledge, or by members of the group feeling disconnected.

Lack of feedback can cause dilemmas about change in many different ways. For example, lack of external feedback—in this case, lack of feedback from the clients and from the people who refer them to the counselling service—creates insecurity about how the organization carries out its primary task. Different people in the organization may, for their own reasons, develop different beliefs about the efficiency of the organization. These beliefs may become competing beliefs that create unproductive conflicts between the members of an organization: for example, about needs for change, goals for change, and how to go about them.

Lack of internal feedback can contribute to the creation and perpetuation of incorrect beliefs about different individuals and work groups within the organization, informal power structures obstructing the formal power structures, and other dynamics that cause resistance to change and the system to become stuck and eventually reduce its productivity.

As the dynamics of the internal and external feedback systems are interdependent, changes in one might further changes in the other. Therefore, to help a system change you might start with one or the other, or work with both. The choice should depend on an analysis of which is the easiest, quickest, and most lasting way to get the system to solve its dilemmas and get unstuck. The important point is to facilitate the flow of feedback, thus making it possible to move to higher levels of belief—from content to process—and from competing beliefs to a negotiated reality. This again will facilitate the creation of new relationships within the system.

Relating this to the request of the counselling group, to my limited knowledge of its history and structure, and to my experience of the mechanisms that often are at work in the kind of volunteer work the members of the counselling service were doing, I decided to base the plan for the course on the following hypotheses about possible dilemmas:

1. That the request itself expressed a dilemma, namely a wish from the staff members to do their work better than they thought they were doing it, at the same time having a feeling of not knowing how to use their resources well enough. I thought that their dilemma probably stemmed mainly from a lack of internal and external feedback and, perhaps, from underestimating themselves and each other because they were fairly inexperienced. This issue may have become pressing because: (a) the older staff members had been working in the counselling service for a long time without getting any systematic feedback that could create the basis for systematic development of skills; (b) many new and inexperienced staff members were starting at the time, and the more experienced staff members felt responsible for the development of the newcomers' skills; (c) the evening unit had been working long enough for the two groups to feel the need to know more about each other's way of working.

2. That the staff members, on the one hand, were mainly motivated to work in the counselling service for two reasons—namely, learning and using therapeutic and therapy-related skills—and doing so in a satisfying social climate, free of the mechanisms involved in paid work. But that the cooperation, the exchange of experiences, and the (mutual) development of skills in both units of the counselling service, on the other hand, might be jeopardized for two reasons: (a) the large turnover in staff mem-

bers and their different levels of information about the counselling service and its history making them feel unconnected;
(b) the fact that the service now consisted of two separate units
with relatively little communication and information about each
others' activities, that is, breaches in the feedback flow within
the system as a whole. The two units had existed side by side
long enough for each of them to develop their own cultures and
set beliefs about the culture of the other unit: this had already
resulted in conflict.

3. That the counselling service had developed a culture that in
some ways hampered the process of learning and change, because it inhibited individuals from contributing some of their
individual knowledge and skills. Doing things the way they
have always been done gives staff members a feeling of competence and security. New staff members adapt to these ways of
doings things (i.e. to the existing culture) and obtain a feeling of
belonging. But continuing the traditions may also cause frustration. In the counselling service, these tendencies may have been
reinforced by the insecurity caused by a new unit having started
up and by both units getting many new staff members.

These dynamics are often at work when an organization has existed over a period of time, especially if it does not get systematic
feedback and lacks experience and knowledge that could further
development. The latter was the case with the counselling service,
most of its staff members being fairly inexperienced and unsure of
themselves. Furthermore, the counselling service did not have any
structures that encouraged the systematic sharing of individual experience, knowledge, and skills that were not already a part of its
beliefs and culture. At this point, most older staff members probably felt that they were repeating themselves.

The request was to develop ways of using the resources of the
counselling service optimally. To ensure this, it was necessary for
the members to feel connected to the service and get a better knowledge of its resources. I therefore assumed that it would be helpful if
the course contained activities that examined the beliefs and culture
of the service, improved the common level of information and
knowledge, developed ways of ensuring the use of individual re-

sources, and created ways of ensuring internal and external feed-back loops. All this, I hoped, would help the staff members to move from a situation characterized by competing realities, to a common negotiated reality.

Using these goals as guidelines in the plan I conceived for the course was meant to ensure the sharing of information and beliefs in the group and to help people already during the process of the course to get connected to the group as a whole. It also gave me a possibility to compensate for my lack of prior information about the dilemmas of the group by exploring and correcting my hypothesis along the way, and to make subsequent necessary changes in the plan.

To further a process of helpful change, the course was also to contain a final phase in which possibilities for change were to be examined with regard to possible gains and losses and the changes themselves planned and evaluated.

The course was to take place on two separate days with approximately a month between them and to last ten hours in all. The plan for the course was not mailed to the participants but was to be introduced at the start of the first day.

CONTENT OF THE COURSE

The start of the course was structured around:

1. *Work in pairs, who were to interview each other about their respective reasons for wanting to improve the work of the counselling service, what they thought was functioning well/less well, and what they were dissatisfied with.*

The pairs were composed of one staff member from the day unit and one from the evening unit, and, when possible, an old and a new staff member were put together. This structure was chosen because of my hypothesis that new members of the staff might feel disconnected from old members, and the day and evening units from each other.

The new staff members whose knowledge of, and experience with, the counselling service was limited were also asked to talk about their fantasies about the service and/or experiences from similar work. These interviews lasted for approximately an hour.

2. *The pairs then communicated the contents of their talk to the large group. Central themes were noted on the board for later use. This plenary session made it possible for me to get some more information about the background for the request, and for the group members to share beliefs about the counselling service.*

Some of the central themes were dissatisfaction with:

• The lack of communication between the subgroups, not using each others knowledge well enough

• Not knowing how the teams in the two subgroups work

• Knowing too little about their own effectiveness with clients

• Not using effectively enough the methods they had acquired.

Themes of satisfaction were:

• The social climate in the subgroups

• A feeling that new staff members were made to feel welcome.

This session took a little over an hour.

The new staff members said that the exercise had made them feel more visible and made it easier for them to formulate what they could contribute to the counselling service. Everyone felt they had got to know each other better, and that the exercise had helped them to start concentrating on the work of the day.

3. *The same pairs interviewed each other about the context and structure of the counselling service and their own conception of its goals. Each pair was to describe beliefs about: (a) The context, that is the external relations of the counselling service; for example, to the community centre that housed its offices and the influence of these relations on their work. (b) The internal structure; that is, for instance, the formal and informal relations between the two units, the formal and informal structures in the units, and the effect that these had. The time spent on the exercise was about an hour.*

The reason for this exercise was to heighten the common level of information and awareness of the system of which they were all a part, show reasons for being stuck due, for instance, to differences in beliefs or to possible differences in the understanding of the goals of the counselling service, give me necessary information for the further process, and provide a common framework for exploring possible changes, and gains and losses in an eventual process of change.

4. *A follow-up meeting with the entire group with a presentation of the discussions that had taken place in the subgroups about the structure of the organization and its goals.*

Some of the themes that emerged were:

*   the structure of the counselling group and its internal and external relations
*   the experience of a lack of awareness of and feedback from external relations, a lack of knowledge about and feedback from the other unit
*   a list of beliefs and wishes about goals

These themes were then discussed from the point of view of breaches in the existing feedback process, how these were related to the existing structure, and the possibility of developing feedback loops.

Seen as a whole, these themes were placed at the start of the course, partly as a compensation for the fact that they had not been discussed thoroughly before the request had been accepted, and partly to heighten the awareness of the individuals and the groups as to their reasons for wanting to work with the question of better use of their resources .

The intention was to start a feedback process concerning the beliefs, in the system, that would facilitate a process of change. Another intention was to introduce concepts that could be helpful in analysing the connection between, on the one hand, structure and goals and, on the other, the actual use of the resources of the individuals and the group. The programme of the first day ended at this point.

SOME REACTIONS TO THE COURSE

I received a surprise at the beginning of the course. At the presentation of the programme, all the muddle about the contents of the two days surfaced. The day unit, which was the subgroup I had had no contact with, had apparently wanted something much more traditionally learning-oriented with a teacher lecturing and/or had wanted to be taught concrete therapeutic skills.

Some time was spent during which the participants discussed back and forth what had been said and by whom at the two meetings at which the request for consultation had been considered.

The discussion more or less split the group in two: the day unit and the evening unit. There was a tendency for the evening unit to "defend" their supervisor's interpretation of the request and to express excitement about going through the proposed process, and for the day unit to be more sceptical. After some more time spent explaining and discussing the ideas behind, and the methods of, the course as it had been designed, it was decided to go ahead as planned.

Very quickly, the participants seemed to become engaged in the process and to be enjoying themselves. People who did not know each other were talking together during the breaks, and the day and evening units were mingling.

At the end of this first day, there was a common evaluation of the process. Nobody was entirely negative, most were quite positive, and some were enthusiastic. These types of reactions were common to both the day and the evening unit and to new and old staff members, although there was a tendency for new members to be the most enthusiastic.

The content of the feedback was that they had learnt more about the counselling service; felt more connected, more as one group instead of two separate units; were more aware of dilemmas and issues in the organization; and were looking forward to working with change. A few people felt that some of the issues that we had worked with were not new to them. And almost all the members of the day unit said that they had had a hard time at first getting into the work, because it had been so different from what they had expected, but that the process after that had been very satisfactory. I was satisfied: the course was a success—I thought!

Afterwards nearly everyone went out for a drink together, which is something they do not usually do.

Some time later I was contacted by a member of the evening unit and told that the day unit had decided they were dissatisfied with the process, felt they had not learned anything, and wanted a written programme for the following Saturday, so that they could be sure that what had been agreed on the first time would also be carried out.

I was puzzled about this change in attitude. The members of the evening unit interpreted it as a result of pressure from some of the old members of the day unit, who were seen as trend-setters. I had no way of judging this hypothesis. But I felt that old members of the day unit, who seemed to be more interested in a course that consisted mainly of more traditional teaching, might have been made to feel insecure by a course that challenged the established way of doing things in the counselling service.

I mailed a programme to the participants and had my doubts about the possible success of the next session. I saw their request for a programme partly as an understandable reaction to their surprise about the actual content of the first session. But in the light of the turnabout in their attitude towards their actual experience of that session, I feared that the request also expressed a lack of confidence in me, which would influence in a negative direction their engagement in the work during the second session. I felt somewhat at a loss about how to deal with it, except for starting up the second session with a discussion of the change in their attitude.

Accordingly, the second day started with a brief discussion of the change in attitude towards the process that had taken place since the last session. Since nobody could explain the change concretely, this discussion left me uncertain as to the reasons behind the change. But some animosity was noticeable between the two groups. Also, the day-unit staff members whose reaction had been partly negative after the first session had become more negative, and the ones who had been positive or mainly positive were silent in the present discussion. My tentative hypothesis was that the change had something to do with a competitive situation between the two units and with the relations between the staff members of the day unit. I did not know how to work directly with these problems in the given situation. I therefore relied on the hope that talking about their dissatisfaction had made the participants open enough to be able to benefit from the rest of the session. I also expected that the changes resulting from the session would initiate changes in these problems.

After this discussion, the plans for the day were agreed on and the group started working again, apparently without restraint.

The course continued in much the same fashion as on the first day; that is, each of the themes mentioned below was initially prepared by the participants interviewing each other about it in pairs (different ones), or discussing it in small groups. This was followed by a discussion of the themes that thus emerged in a plenary session. A plenary session was also used to decide which changes were to be made, how to implement them, and how to follow them up.

The themes worked with were:

- Wishes for change
- Suggestions for change—for example, changes in the relations to clients, other counselling services, internal structure, and so forth
- Gains and losses for individuals, for the unit, for the counselling service as a whole, resulting from subsequent changes
- Planning changes and following up on changes

These themes had been chosen mainly because they had emerged during the last session. The theme of "gains and losses" was chosen because the Danish seminars had made me aware that estimating and sharing conceptions of and feelings about possible gains and losses for an organization and its members, as a result of change, was an important aspect in the process of change itself. It minimizes the risk of unnecessary or inexpedient change and facilitates change in general by, among other things, actively involving everyone in the process.

The theme of planning change was chosen because the participants had asked for it. How to follow up changes was discussed because they felt that it was necessary for them to make sure that changes would be carried out and evaluated.

My role during the day was the same as it had been on the first day. I coordinated the exercises, gave instructions, wrote keywords from the group work on the blackboard when the small group shared the results of their work with the whole counselling service, and helped the participants organize and analyse the information they were gathering for each other in a systemic way, using the concepts I described at the beginning of the chapter.

An example of this was that, at the plenary on suggestions for change, I helped the participants sort out which suggestions had to do with developing structures to facilitate feedback loops, and which had to do with developing methods of obtaining concrete knowledge that was needed in their practice.

At the end of the day, the process and content were again evaluated as positive by the participants, although there was a markedly flatter and less enthusiastic feeling this time.

It was agreed to spend one evening three months later to follow up the process of change.

UNHEEDED WARNING LIGHTS
AND THE MOTIVATION OF THE CONSULTANT

Seeing retrospectively what happened, I had three important thoughts in the process leading up to the actual "course", each of which constituted an important warning light. I did not heed any of them, and that caused some of the muddles and dilemmas described above.

1. *When I was presented with the request, my first thought was that I would like to do the job with another person. This was, unfortunately, not possible. Taking on the task without having a co-consultant, being alone, put more pressure on me. It made it less likely that I would heed my own warning lights, because I had nobody to discuss them with . It also made it impossible for me to become aware of pitfalls that for one reason or another were not visible to me.*

Since I was very unfamiliar with the systemic method of consultation, having another person trained in that way of working might have made me feel more secure, made me more open to spotting dilemmas, and given me the opportunity of putting those dilemmas into words and finding possible solutions. It might also have given me better chances of correcting possible mistakes and learning along the way. In general, one could say that being on my own with the task made it less enjoyable and more stressful.

I had originally accepted the task for the pleasure of exploring the systemic method in practice; however, since my general situation at the time of the course was very stressful, my motivation for spending time and energy on it was greatly reduced.

2. *My second thought at the presentation of the request was that there was a problem concerning the context of the request, namely my direct relations as a supervisor to the evening unit, and my lack of relationship to the day unit. In carrying out the request, I was neither an internal nor an external consultant. I was like a semi-detached garage belonging to one part of a two-family house. I did not reflect thoroughly on my position in the system and its possible consequences, possibly because it might have meant that against my wishes I would have had to give up the thought of carrying out the task.*

The initial muddles about the content of the request and the way it had been communicated to me—namely, through one member of the evening unit—should have made me worry, get more information directly from the day unit, analyse the new information, and act on it.

3. *My third thought, especially as the date of the course drew nearer, was that I did not want to do the course at all. I had too many pressures in my life at the time. The pressure resulted in my not taking care of possible problems when I saw them coming up. For example, I let myself be reassured by my contact person, who was a member of the evening unit, about possible disagreements between the two units over the contents of the request. It was easier that way. I would not have to arrange extra meetings in an otherwise busy life. The whole course had simply become too much trouble.*

It seems to me that a central issue in what went wrong in the process of accepting this request and carrying out the task was failing to heed the warning lights in my mind.

Some of the reasons for that were to be found in my muddled and unreflected motivation for taking on the request. Apart from the chance to practice systemic consultation, I was also feeling flattered that the subgroup that I supervised had suggested me, and I did not want to let them down. Another part of my motivation was the excitement of doing other kinds of work—and work in a different setting than my usual job allows for.

The quality of the consultant's motivation is often a very important part of the context of the process of accepting a request and of carrying out a consultation process. It is, unfortunately, also a rarely examined part of that context, even though it may have considerable influence on the course of action taken and on the resulting events.

PUTTING KNOWLEDGE INTO PRACTICE

Part of my motivation for taking on the task was, as mentioned earlier, wanting an opportunity to put into practice what I myself was learning at the Danish seminars on systemic consultation. That reduced my sensitivity to certain aspects of the request. It made me much too focused on concepts and methods that I had learned recently, instead of listening to the signals that were coming from the group. One of these overlooked signals may have been that the group all along kept calling the "course" a course, although they, according to my knowledge, had agreed on a request for a "consultation". Had I been less interested in using my own newly acquired skills, and more interested in listening to the group, that fact alone would have made me wonder whether we were all heading in the same direction.

My experience is that wanting to practice methods that you have recently acquired on your own can be a very problematic motivation for taking on a task, especially a process-oriented consultation. The essence of process-oriented consultation is analysing and working with the needs of a system of individuals at a given time, and they may not at all correspond with the particular wishes of a consultant-in-training. Moreover, newly acquired skills are often handled rigidly and without much sensitivity to the needs of the system in question.

INTERNAL/EXTERNAL CONSULTANT

I was in no way a "neutral" consultant, but already a part of the system of the counselling service.

The two subsystems of the counselling service, the day unit and the night unit, had a history of occasional mistrust and misunderstandings. Seen from the point of view of the day unit, I was a part of the evening unit and therefore risked being included in whatever judgements might be passed on it.

The members of the evening unit felt that the day unit saw them as a somewhat anarchistic group of people who did not take their responsibilities seriously enough, especially not the common communication, administrative, and decision-making tasks. I was worried that my having "misunderstood" the request and not sent out a programme in advance was seen as an example of just such a failure to assume *my* responsibilities.

The evening group, on their side, felt that the day unit was somewhat too rigid and judgemental. I did not want to adopt their view uncritically, which may have made me blind to the possibility that they may have been right in this belief.

Being a part of the system myself, the probability that I would adopt these beliefs was greater than if I had been an external consultant. Trying not to be to influenced by them, I think I shut my eyes to them, when I should have faced these beliefs, analysed them, and planned the course in such a way as to give the participants a better chance of dealing with them.

Having the above-mentioned beliefs about each other seems, according to my experience, to be quite usual in volunteer organizations made up of an old staff group and a group of newcomers. The mechanisms that further these beliefs are often that the old group has done the hard work in building the organization, and the new group has the freedom to enjoy the fruits of that labour and be more relaxed and experimental, which again might worry the old group.

Seen from the perspective of the evening unit, I was not a neutral person either, being their supervisor, and therefore a person in whom they had placed their trust, on whom they were dependent. That was probably the single most important reason why I did not cancel the contract at a point where it would have been reasonable to do so. I simply did not want to risk jeopardizing my relations to the evening unit.

Not being neutral probably also brought about other dilemmas and difficulties. Some of these became clear by the very different reactions of the two groups when the course started. Whatever the evening unit had expected at first, they were in no way as surprised by the plan as the day unit. They had asked me about it several weeks before it was carried through. I thought the day unit was just as well informed. That certainly proved not to be the case. Not only were my relations to the evening unit much closer than to the day unit, but I had not even made sure that the feedback loops between the two units and between me and the day unit were properly established.

A PROBLEM IN MOVING FROM INTERNAL TO EXTERNAL CONSULTANT

As I see it, some of the pitfalls I landed in originated from my moving from being an internal consultant, with a designated role with certain beliefs attached to it, to being an external consultant whose task it is to look at a process.

My hypothesis is that the strength of the negative reactions from the day unit and the evening unit's "defensive" behaviour and protection of me was at least partly a result of their relations to each other, and of my position in the system of the counselling service as a whole. The members of the evening unit were probably trying their best to protect their "alliance" with me. Moreover, they reacted to what they experienced as a repetition of what they previously and repeatedly had interpreted as the patronizing and critical attitude of the day unit.

The day-unit's reaction to the course was partly a reflection of their opinion of the evening unit. As they apparently regarded the members of it as somewhat irresponsible, they may not even have expected them to be capable of transmitting a request for a course on a theme everybody seemingly had agreed on. That opinion probably also reflected on me, as supervisor of the evening unit.

EVALUATION

I have summarized in these pages some of the worst mistakes I made and left out what might have been more satisfactory parts of the process; as a result, this has given a somewhat lopsided impression of the results.

The process may very well have, at least for a time, increased the negative expectations the two units had towards each other and may therefore have reinforced their difficulties in cooperating. On the other hand, the consultation may not have been as much of a failure as it might seem from these pages.

One of the reasons for dissatisfaction given by older members of the day unit was that they already knew about some of the dilemmas that became apparent during the two days, and had begun to plan change. Most of the people who expressed dissatisfaction were also those who may have felt most insecure about change since they were the ones who had helped to create the structures in the first place. In spite of their dissatisfaction, the course may have helped the counselling service as a whole to get a clearer and shared understanding of these dilemmas and their causes, and may thereby have facilitated helpful change.

Another reason for dissatisfaction, again from the same people, was that they did not get what they had expected. But frustration does not always mean you do not learn something, although it may mean that you have a hard time realizing it, and it may at least for a while inhibit you in using what you learned for relevant change. Realizing that they learned something and/or admitting it might in this case have been especially difficult for the people who had expressed dissatisfaction because they were also the ones whose beliefs and ways of doing things seemed to be challenged the most by change. They may have felt insecure in handing over responsibility, and even more so because it was being facilitated by the supervisor of the evening unit of which they seemed sceptical.

One way, in the future, of avoiding some of the problems I ran into is to place a lot more emphasis on the process around the request. It is important to make sure that everyone is well informed and that there is agreement about the contents of the request and about the way it is carried out. It may also be important to discuss in advance which needs and whose needs are met by the consultation. In this case, it was even more important that everything was clear between me and the day unit, since I already had a relationship with the evening unit and could communicate with them without making special arrangements to do so.

Another way of steering clear of some of the dilemmas I was confronted with is simply not to accept a request for consultation where I will be an internal as well as an external consultant. Having this dual role creates many problems that are very difficult to handle. However, if for whatever reason one does decide to take on such a job anyway, it is helpful to discuss the issue with the participants in advance.

A follow-up is planned but has not yet taken place. However, the evening unit has told me that some of the planned changes have been made and are working to the satisfaction of both units, and that the atmosphere in which common tasks are being carried out is friendlier and more open. The day unit has complimented them on their contribution. They themselves feel that the day unit has become more flexible in their cooperation. This feedback gives the impression that the course was at least partly successful in facilitating change, probably because the process made the individuals in the two groups more visible to each other so that beliefs were changed and became more varied. Some of the structural changes that have been made are changes that enhance such a development and support the flow of feedback.

I, as a consultant, have learned a few important lessons in the process:

- take your time
- check your own motivation
- check the request, its sources, and its background
- make sure information is passed to all involved
- analyse your position in the system and its possible influence on the process of consultation

CHALLENGES BY THINKING SYSTEMICALLY

I have worked for several years with systemic thinking—among other things, in a family counselling service—and I have done some, although not much, consultation work within a frame of reference that in some ways resembles systemic thinking. My previous knowledge and experience thus blends in with ways of thinking introduced at the Danish seminars. It is therefore difficult to say exactly how I was influenced by the seminars: that is, it is difficult to say what I would have done or thought differently if I had not attended them.

But my daily work at the family counselling service, and most of the other jobs I have had, had not given much time or space for theoretical thinking and the exploration of theoretical concepts in practice. This meant that I often worked in a "semi-conscious" way, acting more on experience than on precise analysis formulated on the concepts of a specific theory.

Attending the seminars, doing the course for the counselling service, and formulating some of my thoughts for this chapter have given me that possibility. Doing this I become aware, once again, that having clear concepts helps in analysing a situation more quickly and more precisely. Getting into the habit of using some of the key concepts of systemic thinking in the field of consultation will, I believe, help me avoid some of the pitfalls I have described above.

Using *systemic* concepts in consultation work has, seen from my point of view, the advantage that they help analyse the development of the relations and structures of an organization instead of just describing the formal structure. Systemic analysis also helps focus on the interdependence of these two aspects and the way the task of the organization is carried out. Other theories/methods often focus primarily on the individuals, or on the structure of the organization, and/or on the setting within which it operates.

Working exclusively with the needs of the individuals will in most cases not bring about the changes necessary for the organization to carry out its tasks in a satisfactory way.

Working exclusively with the structures of an organization disregards the fact that these structures are carried by human beings, who have vital knowledge about their own organization. When that knowledge is not used, one may create new structures that do not meet the needs of the individuals in the organization, and who will therefore actively or passively oppose change or suffer unnecessarily by being disconnected.

The systemic way of thinking links these interdependent aspects and makes it possible to analyse how they influence each other, create dilemmas for the individuals and the organization, and inhibit or facilitate significant change. This again makes it possible and necessary to work with methods that make individuals on all levels of an organization participants and agents of change, thereby facilitating and consolidating relevant change.

One of the challenges to the professional who wishes to work with systemic consultation is that, in a way, one has to give up the glorious and secure role of the expert for the more humble role of an interviewer and facilitator. One does not present the answers to problems, but the ways of working with dilemmas. Making potential clients understand that this way of thinking and working can be helpful is another challenge.

One may initially also feel more insecure because you never know quite where the process will take you and the other participants. One therefore has to improvise along the way and cannot have the comfort of having prepared everything beforehand. One is no longer the expert displaying one's prowess but is sharing expertise and responsibility with the other participants in the process.

With growing experience, I think the feeling of insecurity will be minimized, and sharing the responsibility with participants will take some weight off one's shoulders. One will therefore become more focused on the process than on how one performs as an individual. Feeling insecure, as a result of my limited experience with this kind of work, was one of the aspects that influenced my own process and its consequences in the consulting task described above.

By not taking the more customary expert role, one may also make some clients feel uncomfortable, particularly those who expect you to come up with simplified theory and instructions on how to act. They feel that you as the expert should take over the responsibility and do the work for them, not with them. This, I think, was also one of the problems that arose in the process described in this chapter. Here the challenge is to become able to make clients understand the dynamics of systemic consultation and the possible gains they may bring about.

Many consultants today are, in one way or another, internal consultants. Working systemically as an internal process consultant is difficult for many reasons. One of these is that, to be as effective as possible, you have to work with the beliefs, hidden agendas, and informal structures of an organization. These in themselves are explosive themes in staff groups, and they can become even more sensitive if the consultant is a part of the same system. This was the reason I avoided some of the sensitive aspects of these themes in my work with the counselling service. There was, for example, the question of competition between the day and the night units, and the possibility that hidden agendas and informal power structures in the day unit may have been partly responsible for the change in attitude towards the process.

Another challenge, then, to future systemic consultants and courses in consultation might be to explore ways of dealing with this dilemma.

CHAPTER 9

To see the world anew

Inger Dræby

I n this chapter I describe how I have moved into systemic thinking, and how this process has influenced me. The first part of the chapter deals with the theoretical approach, beginning with my encounter with the concept of neutrality; in the second part I give an example of how I have applied systemic thinking in a consulting situation. My learning process has been one of going from theory to practice. The theory has been immensely fascinating, but it was not until I took it out into real life that I discovered how powerful the theory and the technique are.

THEORY
Discovering neutrality

During the Danish seminars, what first struck me in connection with the systemic approach to consultancy was the *concept of neutrality*—a method that helps the consultant avoid taking sides, exactly the pitfall into which I had often stumbled and which I equally often had recognized as sterile.

I remember once being with a group of salespeople and their management team. We were working with communications, and one of the sales representatives made quite a strong verbal attack on a colleague. I had them talk about this, one at a time—listening and rephrasing what they had heard, and it seemed to me that we were on the right track when suddenly one of the managers broke in, saying, "Now, let's not get into any kind of sensitivity training here". I got stuck immediately, turned my attention to the manager, trying to calm him down. I sided with his defensiveness—and lost contact with what was going on there and then and with the rest of the group.

When I first heard about "neutrality", I did not understand the implications—I was merely attracted. I have now reached a point where I can describe neutrality as a position in which I keep an equal distance/proximity to all involved parties—by letting all points of view come forward without categorizing them according to their validity. One point of view is not more correct than any another. They are all versions of reality that in equal degree sustain a framework within which the parties act.

It follows that preserving neutrality in consultancy work means avoiding adhering to one version of "reality"—but, instead, being a catalyst that allows the coming forth and explicit meeting of different versions. Each and every one of us acts according to what we perceive and define as reality. No two persons have the same perception of reality, which in practice makes room for an infinite number of misunderstandings. The successful consultation is often a case of uncovering perceptions and systems of beliefs that guide individual acts—that is, the possibility of "matching" concepts of reality, thereby creating new views and perspectives.

Applying this to the situation with the sales group I described would mean that what I could have done differently was to acknowledge the input from the manager, asking him to have a little patience in the first place, turn back to the two sales reps to have them finish their conversation—and then investigate what the manager's perception of the situation was. I could further have asked for input from other group members—either about their view on the character of the session or about what they saw to be the consequences of the manager's outburst. In this way, new information

about the group's communicative pattern could have been produced.

Systemic theory has from the start seemed to promise a solution
to the biggest problem I experienced in my consultancy—getting
involved and taking sides. And the promise was kept—but simultaneously I was presented with a new and even greater problem. I
learned how to stay neutral, but in that same process I discovered
the anchor to which I had hitherto clung in my consultancy: the
cause-and-effect way of thought—or, in systemic language, linear
thinking. So my dilemma was heightened and raised new questions
of a disturbingly existential nature—namely, the necessity of alter-
ing my way of thinking.

Abandoning truth—discovering relations

Trying to acquire systemic thinking has caused considerable mental
anguish to a point close to physical pain. It has felt as though the
brain was being turned upside down—it was almost tangible how
in the process the customary trains of thought were deconstructed.

I have found that systemic thinking is not something that is just
put on top of what you already know—it is a restructuring not only
of acquired knowledge but of the way information is processed, of
the entire thought process.

It is not possible to work systemically with *the* problems, *the*
case—only with aspects of the relational system in which one
moves. There is no Truth. What can be worked on are the different
perceptions of "the problem" or "reality" of the persons involved.
The consultant is not there to be the expert ("the mouthpiece of
Truth") but to create a process that will bring about change in the
relations between the involved parties. The task is to make it clear
how different views and standpoints interact and define the playing field of the group in question.

The absence of Truth in systemic thinking is both liberating and
frightening. Liberating because one is allowed to throw off the yoke
of expertise; frightening because the options available are limitless.
Developing the ability to contain many versions of reality requires
confidence in the fact that my identity as a consultant does not
depend on which opinions I have. This is the inner dilemma. It

corresponds with the outward dilemma about the role expectancies others have for the consultant.

To acquire a systemic way of thinking means to deconstruct the customary way of thinking—above all, the idea that things can be defined by themselves; that is, that a problem can be mapped and analytically defined as *Ding an sich* [the thing in itself]. Systemic theories applied in consulting operate with *das Ding für uns* [the thing as we see it] and with the practical consequences of this view.

The unconscious *Ding an sich* way of thought underlying my usual approach implies the concept that it is possible to find *the* problem—as the cause of the situation that one desires to change. System theories characterize this view as linear thinking and offer in its place a circular view. In the traditional way of thought, the boundaries of a phenomenon are the end of the story—while according to systemic thinking they are the phenomenon's points of contact with other, larger systems that interact with the phenomenon. Thus, the context helps to define the phenomenon—this is circularity. Every single phenomenon leads to another and can only be understood through its specific relation to this. Where traditional analysis reduces a set of problems, systemic circular questioning opens the set of problems—and in principle this opening is infinite.

I have conducted many sessions under the banner of "problem-solving", during which I have often thought myself able to see clearly what was *the* problem. Revealing this to the people who owned the problem has, however, been of little use. By and by it has become clear to me that it is far more interesting and helpful to look at the relation between the problem and its owners. When a manager says "This employee does not fit socially into my group, but I can't bring up the problem because it's an emotive issue", then *the* problem could be identified as the emotional constitution of the employee or of the manager. If so, the manager would have to choose between this employee and the rest of the group, given that the emotional constitution of a person is not something that can be changed overnight. But looking at the situation from a different perspective, one could ask, "What is the relationship between privacy and availability in this group?"—based on the hypothesis that both the employee *and* the manager are struggling to keep intact their (personal or professional) boundaries and that this struggle can for some reason not be brought out into the open in the group.

The point about this different approach is to move the attention from "the issue" to the relations that produce and maintain it. And this is what is so difficult. Coming from a traditional (reductionistic) cause-and-effect way of thought, it is not possible to *think* one's way into systemic thinking—simply because systemic thinking means a cancellation of this same way of thought. The mental movement in acquiring systemic thinking is not direct, focused, limiting, "right-into" as is traditional thinking. The movement is round about, circling, defocusing, opening. One has to create—and accept to be in—a place where customary ways of thought have no validity. Not knowing, not-understanding, letting oneself float along—that is the necessary mental attitude when the perspective shifts from linear to circular thinking.

There are practical consequences attached to which perspective is used. Ways of thought are not innocent or neutral. They structure perceptions, decide what can be recognized and what cannot—what you see as being inside or outside the limits of reality. If a landmap is used to illustrate a person's concept of reality, then ways of thought represent the geodetic principles that are used for making the map. Berit Sander's contribution in Chapter 6 shows how different geodetic principles result in different attitudes and ranges of action on behalf of the consultant.

PRACTICE

Entering systemic consultation

In my early stages of learning systemic consultation, I became totally confused about which side of the system to grab hold of. Where does one start when everything is interrelated? The freedom of choice that opened challenged my courage, causing quite a paralysis of action. It was not until I realized that I was running around in circles like a chicken without a head that I decided that the only way to progress was to become practical.

It is necessary to let go of the idea that theory and method can be mastered without trying it out in practice. Thus, it is necessary to be willing to fail. And the courageous ones are rewarded: trying in real life to work systemically provides a qualitative leap in understanding of what it is all about. And the leap is not limited to understanding: it gives new self-confidence in relation to all the mental tremors of the learning process.

It goes faster through the back door

The big landslide, then, occurred when I tried the systemic concept out in practice. It was like entering through the back door—much quicker than the front door, which is constructed of a heap of words that in fact are meant to prevent you from entering.

I have been working as an internal consultant to a company for some years and have moved, from a teaching position, more and more into consultation. The organization from which the following case is taken is a sales subsidiary of a large international company.

I was asked to help a sales team that had problems working together. It was the group manager who had approached me, and in contracting we agreed that it was necessary to have a frank and open discussion about what was going on, a discussion in which the manager himself was not supposed to be protected. I had known the group for some years and was aware that, although there had been some turnover, the problems remained unchanged. It was my hypothesis that the problem lay in the inability to discuss the manager's leadership style and bring about change through open critique.

My normal method would be to start collecting data: "What do *you* see as the problem? and you? and you?" Writing it all up on the blackboard. Reducing the items into categories, making precedences, diving into them, finding possible solutions. All of which I would now describe as a front-door strategy.

The front door of a house is what you show the public. A lot of Danish provincial towns are famous for their beautifully carved and painted front doors. They are normally kept locked, even during the day. The back door you do not see. To reach it you have to go through the backyard (which is surrounded by a fence or a hedge). But this is the open door used by the family and their friends.

Groups with long-standing problems have usually learnt to live with those problems. And—still more important for the consultant—even though the group has problems it is still a group, an intact system trying to preserve itself and its cohesiveness—feeble as it may be—in the face of outside intervention. In other words, it will have ways of presenting itself to the public (i.e. the consultant). The front door is ship-shape, no matter what goes on behind it.

What the group will not reveal are its internal relations—doing so would be much too dangerous (this is a real vicious circle). It is all right for the group to talk about problems, but as something extra-relational, as foreign bodies floating about making life difficult; stories and events as congealed facts. They have long since lost all life, and if you as a consultant let yourself get caught in these stories, you are immediately in a vortex of never-ending causal chains and complicated questions of guilt. This does not mean that there is no life around the problems; there is almost a ritual dance going on that keeps them alive. Individual group members may think of themselves as trying to solve the problems, but their approach to the other members ("If he or she would just change that . . .") has the opposite effect. The interesting thing, therefore, is much more the power that the problem has in the present than how it was created originally.

Trying to approach the relations of a group like this through the front door is bound to be a futile effort. It is staying at the surface, naive, taking everything that is presented to me as a consultant for granted. The only outcome that is produced is a heap of new words; we do not reach the rub. Instead, inspired by the Danish seminars, as an exercise I asked the members of the group to write down, anonymously, their beliefs about the group's hidden agendas. I can think of several reasons why they consented to this:

- *Surprise.* I had not presented a programme; instead, in order to circumvent habitual thinking about structured problem-solving and gain access to creativity, I started out by depicting the sensations of mountain hiking. I took them from the nice and cosy, but narrow, valley up to the top from where they could see far and recognize the structures of the landscape. I told them they felt good about it.

- *The need for structure to provide some security in a situation that everybody expected to become painful.* Dependence on the consultant is always stronger in the beginning of a session, which leads to greater readiness to do as he or she asks.

- *A benevolent attitude towards me as a person.* I have known most of the group members for quite a'while, and they have confidence that I am not out to stab them in the back.

Protests came when they were asked to hand over their notes about hidden agendas. So we discussed their different reactions to being manipulated and used my exercise about hidden agendas as an example. That loosened their tongues, and several were now eager to set the agenda for the day. This we did, in a quite traditional way with items on the blackboard. The list became short, there was nothing new, and the energy in the group faded quickly.

As nobody had any other ideas about how then to spend our time, we resumed working with the notes about hidden agendas. I read aloud randomly from the notes and wrote all the items on the blackboard. That amounted to a long list, forty-five items in all. Here are a few examples:

- to hide weaknesses
- to get recognition (no matter the costs)
- to obtain personal freedom with regard to expenditure of time
- to keep control over one's own work area
- to please one's bosses
- to make friends
- to have fun at work
- to avoid conflict
- to get acceptance from everybody
- to secure one's future (play it safe)

Am I seen? Am I respected? Am I used? Do I get what I need? Those were the questions I perceived behind the many suggestions for the agendas. At this point, I could have chosen the path of talking about those and similar questions, and about whom they most wanted to ask them to, but that was an afterthought.

However, when I sat down contemplating the long list of hidden agendas I just about slid back into my old method. I was thinking: we must systematize all this material a little bit—categorize it or something. But luckily I chose to raise first the question I had prepared—another direct inspiration from the Danish seminars: "Give me three good reasons why it is necessary to have these hidden agendas—or more correctly, why it is necessary to keep them hidden."

These are some examples of what came up in response to this question:

- recognition of the existence of contradictory goals
- fear of having one's motives exposed
- fear of being fired
- fear of creating enemies
- fear of confrontation
- fear of blocking one's career (being looked at as the inevitably cantankerous person)

That was when I had a great revelation: I saw the back door. All reasons for hidden agendas are indeed relational—they stem from the relations between persons in a specific group. They may be determined by competition, exaggerated caretaking, insecurity with regard to ground and cultural rules, and so forth.

With the much shorter list that now materialized (fourteen items in all) we were at the heart of the matter. The procedure of systematizing and categorizing now appeared as a long detour—with a considerable risk of losing one's way, at that.

The driving force behind the hidden agendas was fear—in many shades and many different personal colourings. In this situation, I was not able to establish a direct discussion on the substance of fear—this would have taken us into a confrontative course that I did not feel secure (!) about. However, I hoped that it had now become obvious to the entire group that they could not solve their problems without dealing with their fear—this has after, the event, proven to be true. Individual group members went higher up the hierarchy with their complaints. Although this was also imagined to be a dangerous step, they had decided that it was better to act than to endure. Eventually, the manager was moved to another job.

REAR-VIEW MIRROR REFLECTIONS

Looking back on my learning process, I see how it developed into a kind of spiral: every time I reached an answer to a problem, a new question was raised, which pushed me into further learning. My initial problem was a practical one: how to position myself in a consultation so that I could avoid taking sides and as a result getting stuck. The answer lay in the concept of the "multi-verse" and the shift of focus from "problems" to the relational field that holds and creates problems. This took me into questioning my linear thinking, causing a mental turn-around that almost paralyzed me. The jump into practice got me moving again and showed me both the territory I had gained and some of the new challenges that lay ahead.

The most decisive move in my learning process has been this last one, from thinking to doing. It was through this move that I really *comprehended*—bodily perceived—what the *difference* is. Where earlier on I was striving to reach the final point of explanation and solution, now I am learning to live with openings and the concept of never-ending interrelations.

Do others view it as radically different as I do myself? Certainly not. However, *some* change has been experienced. Feedback I have received from colleagues and clients since I started using a more systemic approach is: "It is much more obvious, now, how different we are from each other. We used to act as though we all saw things the same way." I interpret this as a relief that it is now possible to talk together openly about more things. That the organization can in fact contain much more diversity than it used to believe it could— and can thus prosper from it.

CHAPTER 10

Learning from feedback: long-term consultation to a school

Dodo Astrup

INTRODUCTION

T his is the story about two psychologists and how they were challenged by a task that was novel to them. It is also a story about a learning process. The task was a consultation at a large state school in Copenhagen. The theme presented to us was to improve communication among the staff, especially between the leaders and the teachers. The staff at the school consisted of around thirty persons, including the headmistress and two deputies.

One of the psychologists was leader of the local school guidance service, and the other was a clinical psychologist at the same office. Neither of them, at the time, had had any training in professional consultation. But the clinical psychologist—who is also the writer—was quite experienced in the use of systemic therapy, supervision, and thinking and was currently attending the Danish seminars on systemic consultation. We both wanted to learn more about consultation and systemic theory, so we welcomed this task as an opportunity to engage in a learning process—which hopefully would also help the school. We immediately decided to do a process consultation with a systemic approach. We felt lucky that the

123

time coincided with my participation at the seminars, at which I could get feedback and inspiration. (We felt quite nervous but also enthusiastic about this new job.)

HOW WE GOT THE CONSULTATION TASK

The first contact from the school came in January 1992. We were telephoned by the teacher's representative, who invited us to contribute to a meeting at the school, on the theme of communication. On the telephone it was arranged that we would come to the school beforehand and meet with him and the teachers' committee and the three leaders. Before this first meeting, we received some written material from the school. It was about former arrangements and activities in connection with the school's engagement in bettering its relations and communication. We realized that these attempts went back some ten years. What interested us most, however, was a questionnaire containing a few very short questions about the relations among the staff at the school and proposals to change or better these. The answers revealed very different attitudes among the teachers.

At this very first meeting at the school, we received some important information: the three leaders had all been appointed within the last two years. The shift in leadership had been drastic, because the old headmaster had been very authoritarian, and the new headmistress was much more democratic. But at the same time as she had delegated out more responsibility, she had also been accused of being quite autocratic.

At the meeting, it became clear to us that it had been decided in the teachers' council that we should be hired as consultants, not only for a one-day meeting but for several other days including a weekend. Most but not all of the teachers had agreed to this plan, and some had declared that they felt too tired to participate in such a process. We noted that the headmistress was the person who was best prepared for this meeting, in view of her notes and her up-to-date knowledge. We decided to have a meeting with the whole school just before the summer vacation, where we would present our plan for the coming consultation weekend in September. This would be held at one of the school camps on the coast. It was agreed that we should have a follow-up meeting soon after the weekend.

THE CONSULTATION STARTS:
THE FIRST MEETING WITH THE SCHOOL

So, we had had our first telephone conversation with the referral person and the first meeting at the school, at which our contract was negotiated and agreed upon. We already had enough information for a handful of hypotheses. Now we needed to have a good discussion between ourselves before we planned our first meeting with the whole school. At this time, we came up with some main reflections:

- The agenda had shifted from a day about communication to a consultation for a whole school. And we had just accepted the task! We had accepted because we were curious, and because we wanted to learn—but also because we believed that we had something to contribute with. When we were with the whole group, we wanted to be open about our own communication. That is, we wanted to let everyone know about the contacts we had had with the school, all the telephone calls and the information we had received, so that people could feel safe. (This idealism didn't quite last the whole consultation through!)

- We wanted to make our roles as systemic consultants clear. That meant that we would take care not to get involved in decision-making and responsibility for change as the consultation went on.

- As consultants we would help to bring up and to clarify issues and problems, but we would not decide which topics were the most important to be dealt with. We would engage people to find out for themselves.

- We should be prepared for some resistance and lack of engagement since not all of the teachers had wanted consultation.

- We should deal with our own insecurities and lack of experience. This meant lots of discussions between ourselves in which we could generate ideas, look at the feedback, and revise our thinking.

From the answers to the questionnaire we could see that there was a great split at the school, and that this was between the teachers and the leaders but also between groups of teachers. Our approaches towards changing this were, first of all, to accept differences in opinions, to say things more openly, and to have more openness from the leaders, especially the headmistress.

With this background we went to have our first meeting with the whole school in May 1992. Our primary task at this first meeting was to induce optimism and hope in the school and to declare our attitude as consultants, as agents in their own process of change. We informed the whole group about our contract and about our contacts with the school up to that point. We praised them for their continuous engagement to improve communication at the school and for all their attempts up to now. We told them that we saw a development in these attempts from working with communication in general and addressing external relations to a recognition of the need to focus on their own internal relationships. We pointed out that we saw this as an important change and as a good starting point for the coming consultation. We mentioned the questionnaire, and that we had made a summary of the answers. We had been especially interested in the answers to the last question, which asked for suggestions to better the communication at the school. We conveyed to them that they themselves already had many ideas and suggestions concerning changes in their communication.

At this meeting we were met with a somewhat tired and passive kindness. People were mostly concerned with examinations and the new schedule for the coming school-term. It was difficult to get feedback or any ideas for specific wishes for the coming consultation weekend. They accepted our plan and did not show any concern or need to discuss it with us. We left with a funny sort of empty feeling and some ideas for new hypotheses. Do some people dominate others? Are objections prohibited? Did we forget to listen? Should we have started to ask for feedback instead of presenting a plan?

A WEEKEND WITH SYSTEMIC CONSULTATION

So we found ourselves in the situation of not having any clear feeling about what people really wanted from us. We just sensed a diffuse atmosphere of discontent and a dissatisfaction, which was defined as a conflict between teachers and leaders (mostly the headmistress).

From here we had to make a plan for the weekend. For a start, we made the following reflections:

- We had a hypothesis about many controversies at the school—both old and contemporary.
- We had a hypothesis about the headmistress being a scapegoat.
- We had a hypothesis about a widespread ambivalence: "We work hard to create a better school, but we feel worn-out and don't want to pay the costs for change."
- We wanted to help people reveal some of their dilemmas. In that connection, we also wanted them to discuss their wishes and hopes for the consultation.
- We would try to stay as neutral as possible. We knew that this could be difficult, because we too were part of the school system. We had certain relations, problems, etc. in common. We planned to stay as much to ourselves as possible and to have our own private conferences.
- In our effort to stay neutral, we would take care not to get involved in their stories. We would be careful not to be pressed for engagement and solutions. Instead, we would keep an optimistic attitude and show our belief in their own resources and also point out what the school actually had succeeded with until now. (This turned out to be very ambitious and difficult.)
- We would allocate our own roles, so that one of us at a time would be responsible for a session—or would be the active one. The other would then be free to observe and give feedback.
- We would work with reflective teams, using the "fishbowl" format from the Danish seminars, and open group discussions.
- We would confer about our plan with a more experienced colleague.

As a learning point, much later we asked ourselves whether we had missed something at this point in the consultation—namely, to explore a bit further why the mood had been so low or tired at our first meeting with the whole school. We could have used this feed-back at the start of the weekend and presented it as our dilemma.

But we wanted to pursue the idea that people should be active, should try to formulate their own dilemmas and wishes, and on this basis we made a plan, which we then followed, for the first day. After a short introduction in which we presented ourselves as con-sultants and informed them about our systemic way of working, we repeated the contract and the way it was presented to us: the school wished to improve internal relations and communication, and there were conflicts between teachers and leaders. We gave them feed-back on their answers to the questionnaire. Our résumé of the answers had shown three layers of conflict: teachers/leaders, teach-ers/teachers, and old controversies among groups of them. We told them that we would work with the defined teacher/leader conflict, but that we wanted to explore the two others first, because that might help all of us to understand the first one better. For this pur-pose we introduced an exercise in which they were asked initially to form into subgroups of six persons. Everyone was to write down some ideas and hypotheses about old conflicts at the school, of whatever nature. The six persons in each subgroup then listened to each others' ideas and discussed them. After this they were asked to choose three hypotheses about still existing dilemmas or conflicts to present to the whole group. In the event, this proved to be a very helpful exercise for participants and also for us, because it gave a lot of information about history, about contemporary problems, and about the process of decision-making and how it was handled in the subgroups.

Next came the fishbowl discussion with the whole group. We had each subgroup in turn in the middle to discuss openly in front of their colleagues. We had decided in our plan (1) to acknowledge and support the three hypotheses, (2) to ask about the other hypoth-eses, and (3) to ask them how they had arrived at the three chosen hypotheses. In this way, we tried to keep out of the content and to focus on the process and relations in the subgroups.

People were very eager to get into the "hot seats". It had been a good experience for them in the small groups. The discussions went on freely in the fishbowl setting. Sometimes I would ask questions such as, "What does this mean for you in your daily work?", or "What do you think the others think?", or "How do you think that this blocks the energy today?" We used the large group as a reflecting team. Many persons, including the leaders, said that this afternoon had provided some new and important information. So much information came up about old controversies and about insecurities concerning tasks and responsibilities that at the end of the day we, a little provocatively, reformulated the dilemma at the school as a communication problem between certain groups of teachers. We therefore proposed to take this up the following day instead of the defined conflict between teachers and leaders. But we were met by marked protest from the majority of the teachers.

When the two of us conferred that evening, we were puzzled about this protest. We sensed a certain degree of aggression, some of it directed towards the leaders. The aggression was also apparent from the heated way in which hang-ups about old controversies were discussed. From this day's exercise we learned that people could cooperate quite well in small arbitrary groups and be rather open about problems and conflicts. But we could also see that it was difficult for them to address their dissatisfaction directly. In spite of the positive feedback during the exercise, my colleague and I felt anxious. We also felt too inexperienced to deal with a lot of emotionality in a large group. We therefore chose to "go with the resistance" and to stay with our original plan to deal with the teacher/leader conflict.

For the next day we had planned a "negotiation exercise". This was an exercise in which people would have representatives or advocates to bring forth their wishes and to negotiate for them with representatives from their "opponents". The two "opponents" were the leaders and the teachers. In the first half of the exercise these two groups would be apart with their respective representatives and a consultant, and the task of the representatives would be to listen to their "clients" and to help them bring forth what these wanted to clarify, discuss, say, or ask for—so that the representatives would be able to negotiate on their behalf. In the second part of the exercise, the negotiation discussion between the two groups of representatives would be done in a fishbowl setting with the rest of the staff as a reflecting team. The idea with this exercise was to reveal and deal with conflict in a setting that was not too aggressive and would give the real opponents the opportunity to observe and reflect. We also had an idea that the process of listening as advocates would give some new insight to people. Finally, we chose the exercise because we needed some structured plan at this time of our consultation. We did not feel that we had sufficient tools just to let things happen and deal with them as they arose. We had not foreseen that this would turn out to be an extremely difficult exercise!

In the first part of the exercise, I went with the leaders and their representatives. In a very short time a real quarrel flared up between the leaders and their teacher representatives, in which the teachers accused the leaders and the leaders explained and defended themselves. They completely fell out of their roles. It was an old, seemingly unfinished conflict about a "transference-list" in which teachers might be forced to move to another school, because of an order from the school directorate. I had a hard time trying to get people involved in the exercise. I became confused, not knowing what to do.

I decided to let this situation play itself out. Quite against the plan, I was watching a real teacher/leader conflict in vivo. It was not easy for them in this atmosphere to get back to the task, and it was difficult for these teachers to listen to and be advocates for their leaders. When I later looked back at this, I could see that it was an interesting process, and that I could have used it constructively. For example, I could have helped people to reflect about the process itself. Instead, I became distressed, because I lost control and because I did not know what they were talking about. I thought that it was important that I understood their conflict. In that way I was caught up in the content of their arguments. I did exactly what I had planned not to do! So, it went wrong, because I lost the metaposition and became unable to help them analyse what was going on. It was a very instructive experience for me! From this I learned that it is not so important to know and understand details in a conflict (which is impossible anyway); what is important is to watch the conflict, to analyse the process, and to give people feedback on this. It was a very important learning point for me, and it helped me in my later work with this school.

The group discussion in the fishbowl was slow and unenergetic, mainly because it was difficult for the teachers who were advocates for the leaders to keep their roles. What came up was mostly criticism of and accusations against the leaders—especially the headmistress. So in a way the argument in my small group repeated itself in the fishbowl setting. Because of this we ended this exercise by letting the three real leaders sit in the middle and discuss with a group of teachers, and finally we let the leaders discuss openly among themselves, while everyone listened. Since the idea with the advocates had not really worked out, we also felt that the leaders had not had a fair chance to speak for themselves and openly discuss their problems and answer the accusations. We felt that this was a rather good process, and that it cleared up certain misunderstandings about different details in the conflicts. It also gave the teachers the possibility to listen, to ask questions, and to give feedback. Things came more out into the open. This went quite well, and we wondered what hindered people in their daily lives against giving this sort of feedback. At the end of the day, we concluded in our usual systemic way by acknowledging the way they had engaged themselves in the process, pointing out dilemmas, and asking for ideas for change. We were given a few ideas and also gave some ourselves. We took care to write them all down. We gave the feedback that we saw lack of openness as the greatest dilemma at the school, and we proposed—which other persons also did—that people should try to address their questions, insecurities, and discontent more directly.

This day was a hard one for all of us—but we guessed that it also had been constructive, because the weekend ended in surprisingly good spirit. Before we left, we made plans for a follow-up meeting within the next two months. On our way home we reflected upon our own dilemmas. Why this happiness about the first day? Why was it so difficult to handle the negotiation exercise? What happened? What precisely brought out the aggressions? We had learned that the negotiation exercise was too structured, too stiff— at least in our case. I had the thought that the aggression it stirred up was perhaps a legitimate way to show anger, which actually belonged to the group of teachers. The first day was possibly easier, because it also concerned past history: it was easier to deal with old controversies. We liked the exercise from the first day ourselves and learned that it could be a good way to start a consultation and get people slowly used to openness and process analysis. We were concerned about the leaders, especially the headmistress, and how the near future would be for her. Later we realized that we should have given her more attention and help. This was one of our learning points.

THE FOLLOW-UP MEETING

For the follow-up meeting in November, we planned to stay with the issues of change, and the proposed ideas for change, that we had written down at the end of the weekend consultation. We also wanted to get some feedback on the exercises, the method, and so on. We were concerned about the three leaders, and we would seat them next to each other and next to one of us. Beforehand, we had made the following hypotheses:

- We think that something has changed at the school.
- We think that some teachers actually like the way the headmistress manages her job, but it is against the "culture" to express this.
- The belief at the school is that the headmistress is a bad leader; maybe it is an old belief that is independent of the person.

At the meeting we placed people in a large circle. At the start there was a lot of positive feedback. They felt more openness, and some of the ideas for change had been taken up. Again, people expressed satisfaction with the first exercise. It had contributed to a greater understanding among the teachers. The headmistress said that the weekend had been hard for her, and that it had been difficult for her afterwards. She had felt responsible for the effects of the consultation, and she had had to take care of individuals who needed to talk after the weekend. She had had these conversations together with the teachers' representative. As we sat there we posed questions such as:

- "What has been the most surprising thing that has happened at the school, since we last met?"
- To the teachers: "What have the leaders done differently that you find the most surprising?"
- To the leaders: "What have the teachers done that you find the most surprising?"

In this way we hoped to focus more on process—especially the process of change—than on content.

After the break there was a complete change in the atmosphere. People became angry and accused us of asking questions in a way that prevented them from expressing themselves. Now we were criticized for the weekend and especially for the second exercise. The negotiation exercise had been okay in itself they said, but it brought up too much content, which there was no time to deal with. Some persons said that we had caused a process to start, and that there had not been time to follow it up. But the most serious criticism was about the way we had given space for the leaders at the very end of the consultation, and how we let them speak—both for themselves and in a dialogue with the teachers. Now some of the teachers expressed dissatisfaction with the leaders' behaviour and statements at that time. Some blamed the headmistress for not taking notes during the consultation and for not taking responsibility for the proposed ideas for change. Finally, the headmistress repeated that it had been a very hard weekend for her, and that she had been extremely tired afterwards. She had needed more time. Then she suggested that we should get on now and cope with the discontent that was there.

This turn of events after the break surprised my colleague and me to such an extent that we became somewhat perplexed and unsure of what to do. We did not have much time left at the meeting, so we chose to state that we had listened to them—had heard about their difficulties but also about the positive changes. Then we told them that it had been our plan to pay special attention to the leaders, and that we would continue to do that. We reminded them about the way things had been presented to us from the start— namely, as a conflict at the school between teachers and leaders; that is, between a large group and a very small group. Therefore, we would, as consultants, pay special attention to this smaller group. We would also pay special attention to the role and responsibility of the headmistress.

A bit puzzled, we left the meeting—where it had been decided without discussion that we should continue the consultation. We immediately produced a new set of hypotheses:

- Had there been some hidden agenda at the meeting? There was an ambivalent attitude towards the headmistress: "She is very clever, which is good. But we don't like her to be too clever. We want her to be democratic, but sometimes we want her to take responsibility."

- Was the meeting a picture of the usual way to communicate at the school? First you smile and declare that everything is fine, and then you criticize and attack? If so, this produces insecurity and muddle, which was exactly what we had experienced at the meeting.

- Maybe the aggression against us was an indirect expression of unclear feelings and a split among the teachers themselves.

Later I received the feedback at the Danish seminars that we could have explored questions such as: "What would you have liked to happen?" "What would you like to happen right now?" "What questions would you like us to ask?" These were learning points for us. Another important learning point was the fact that we had not taken enough care of the headmistress and her role as chief. We realize now how important it is to discuss with leaders how they want to be involved in the consultation and to clarify what their responsibility should be in the process of change.

THE IN-BETWEEN PERIOD

It was decided that we would have another weekend consultation the following autumn and a follow-up meeting. Meanwhile I had received some feedback and ideas from the Danish seminars. Both from our experience and from the seminar I had learned that it is important to meet with the leaders alone to discuss their special situation, and to keep news up-to-date. We considered having a meeting with the headmistress alone, but instead we had several telephone conversations with her. We had a meeting with the three leaders a month before the next weekend consultation. We wanted to explore the following questions:

- When there have been changes before at the school, how have they been handled?

- Which dilemmas do you see today at the school? Do you still think that there is a leader/teacher conflict?
- What are your worries for the future?
- How do each of you want to be involved in our weekend consultation?

The feedback we received was that things were going quite well at the school. One change was that the teachers were generally more open and willing to contact the headmistress in matters that were unclear or unsatisfactory. There was still a marked split in groups among the teachers, and there was still a tendency to see the headmistress as autocratic—especially when there were problems. She had a bad reputation with regard to the transference-list of teachers. But the leaders did not experience the conflict between themselves and the teachers as so marked any more. People had striven to realize some of the proposals for change that came up during the consultation weekend. One example was a better procedure at the meetings of the teachers' council. The leaders' foremost concern about the near future was a most realistic fear that for economic reasons one of the deputies would be transferred from the school. Then all of them expressed a wish to participate in the coming consultation on the same terms as the teachers. They wanted to have the freedom to listen and to learn. They gave us positive feedback on our increased attention and on our plan to meet with the three of them shortly after the coming weekend consultation.

PREPARING
THE SECOND WEEKEND CONSULTATION

After this meeting with the leaders, my colleague and I felt that we had a dilemma! We had received ambivalent feedback from the teachers concerning the first weekend consultation. Half a year later, the leaders told us that things were going quite well at the school, and that they had experienced certain positive changes in the interactions. Since a positive process obviously had been started, we wondered if this would be the right time to end the consultation. But then we had been hired for another weekend! Our dilemma was that we did not have any idea about what to do, about what the staff needed now.

Fortunately, the final session of the Danish seminars took place three weeks before the consultation. At the seminar I volunteered to present this case for discussion, with the whole group as a reflecting team. That helped! About the content of the consultation, the advice was that we could let people decide this for themselves. We could let them discuss in small groups what would be important for them to work with now, what they needed our help with, and what changes they wished for. We might ask them to come up with, for example, ten issues to be discussed. The aim was to make them generate ideas in the subgroups. We could ask questions such as, "How can we together define your dilemmas or problems at the school at this time?" We should be careful to phrase our questions so that positive things also came up. For example, we could ask about the good things at the school, what was worth keeping, and what people had in common that was valuable to them. Concerning method, it would be good to have a lot of discussions in subgroups, in which people could feel safe and freer to talk. When we worked with the whole group, we could place the leaders in the middle from time to time and ask them, "What do you think now?" "What do you need to hear more about?" "Is there anything you need to say or clear up now?" We could do the same with groups of teachers. If we were criticized, we could ask what they wanted to happen that was different, or what questions they would like us to ask.

Furthermore, I received feedback from the seminar that it could be important that we as consultants had an awareness of which level of openness we would work at: how much emotionality did we want to come out, and how detailed any confessions and accusations? A great degree of openness might cause a lot of turbulence and a period of instability in the whole system. This might further cause many difficulties for the headmistress to handle. We would bear this in mind as we prepared our questions and statements for the consultation. For this coming weekend consultation, we did not want to have a structured plan as we did the last time. We wanted to be ready to monitor our plan as we went on. We felt that we had better tools now and could allow ourselves greater freedom. From the seminar, I received the advice that we should remember to listen in a positive way, to accept what is there, to use this information and not necessarily challenge it. We should be careful not to be too ambitious: our primary task should be to help them look at themselves. We could bring the old dilemma about leaders and teachers into the session and ask them how they wanted us to help with this now. The idea was to get them involved, to make them talk about it. This would be the learning process—not solving the dilemma. The final advice from the seminar was that we as consultants could talk for a little while about school systems in general and list some of the common dilemmas in public schools in Denmark.

So with this input we made the following plan for the weekend consultation:

1. We would put people in small groups (we would join the three leaders) and ask them to discuss the following issues:

    •   "What should happen at your school in order to say that something has happened?"

    •   "In which way would you experience and express that these two days have been useful?"

    •   "Write down five or ten ideas about what would be important to discuss or clarify. For example, what things are worth keeping and what things are not worth keeping?"

2. We would make a fishbowl discussion with each subgroup in the middle one at a time and the rest as a reflecting team.

3. We would conclude this exercise and this day by writing down the major ideas and issues and give a summary of the day, and possibly clarify formulated dilemmas and interventions and give positive feedback.

4. We had a hypothesis that there was still antagonism among old groupings of teachers—even if this was not so open any more. We devised an exercise in which people could talk together under the safest of circumstances. Each person, including the leaders, should find another person whom they did not know very well or communicate much with in their daily work. People should sit in different rooms in small groups so that they could speak freely with each other in dyads. We asked them to interview each other and to keep strictly to the questions. They were:

    •   "How do you feel working at this school? When do you feel

most competent? Most vulnerable? Most competing? When
do you think that others experience you as most competent,
vulnerable, or competing?"

- "What are your most important alliances—also your covert
alliances?"

- "In which overt or covert manner do you try to influence your
working place? How do you think that others see this?"

- "How can I help you to become better at your job?"

After a time we would ask the subgroups in their different
rooms to discuss together the following:

- "What did I learn from this exercise?"

- "Did I learn something new? Did I get any new insight?"

- "What insight do we get in the group discussing this?"

5. We would end the day in the whole group. We would remember
   to put the leaders in the middle and let them talk about what
   they learned from the exercise. We would be careful to let every
   subgroup mention a few problem areas that could be important
   to work with, and we would write these down. We would end
   the day with positive feedback and a summary of the day.

So with these exercises and questions prepared we actually
made a clear plan for ourselves—just like last time. But we felt different about it. We felt much more ready to let go of the plan. We
felt more experienced and clear about staying in the meta-position.
We also agreed to give each other feedback at the consultation if
one of us "fell in" and got caught in stories or conflicts. We were not
so afraid to improvise, because we had learned to analyse the situations better.

THE SECOND WEEKEND CONSULTATION

The weekend went far better than we had hoped for. There was a
lot of activity, lots of discussions, plenty of ideas, and we had positive feedback on the exercises as well. We could stay with our plan.
All the groups were eager to sit in the middle and talk about their
discussions, when we had the fishbowl setting with the rest of the

staff as reflecting team. It took a long time. Many things came up—among them criticism of the leaders. There were different but also identical ideas for issues that would be important to discuss. It was fun for us to note that it is unusual and surprising for people to be praised and complimented. It is not a very Danish habit. We felt that it had a positive and energizing effect.

There was great satisfaction with the exercise in which two persons interviewed each other and afterwards each room had a group discussion. There had been a great degree of openness in the interviews, and that had caused a different atmosphere of seriousness and attentiveness in the subsequent room discussions.

As on the first weekend consultation, the most important things that came up were information, sorting out that information, and the realization that people could trust each other to clarify things in open discussions—even things towards which there was a negative attitude. They decided to change the procedure at the teachers' council meetings and focus more on the process at these meetings. Also, they found out that they needed a better understanding of the procedures and competencies in the different committees at the school. It was a weekend with a rather open and positive atmosphere, even though some difficult things also came up. We sensed a willingness to understand things and that the staff dared to be more direct in their statements. We were impressed that everybody was still so engaged. We looked forward to the planned follow-up meeting.

EVENTS AT THE SCHOOL
PRIOR TO THE NEXT FOLLOW-UP MEETING

Three weeks later we had a meeting with the leaders. Before that, we had looked closely at the main issues and proposals for change from the weekend. We could see clearly that there was still a great deal of uncertainty at the school. It seemed as though some people were fundamentally unsure about the school's belief system. Some thought that there was a divergence over whether the major value in the educational work was quality or quantity—and that the leaders tended to prefer quantity. This was one of the themes that came up at the consultation weekend, and certain misunderstandings were taken up.

But after this short time we mostly wanted to get feedback from the leaders and ask them if anything new had come up. We also wanted to explore with them how they saw their own responsibilities in the process of change, what they thought the teachers expected of them in this respect, and how we could help them with this.

We received very positive feedback from the leaders. Then they told us they felt that the focus had changed from the headmistress to that of the teachers. The headmistress herself had not felt this so much, and she still sensed that people endowed her with authoritarian motives. She reflected a little upon her own self-perception in this long-lasting atmosphere of mistrust and misunderstandings. One of her most demanding tasks was to make the final decision about when or if a teacher had to be transferred as a result of economic restraints. In this matter there was not even agreement among the teachers. The headmistress expressed that she constantly felt herself to be the scapegoat in this complicated matter.

It was a long and unstructured talk with the leaders, and they obviously used us to vent their feelings. We decided that it was all right for us to take this role, and it did not prevent us from giving and receiving feedback. We had now reached the end of the year, when a lot of things happened rather fast at the school. It all started with a teacher who moved to another school. He was not transferred but had wanted a new position. The history of this particular teacher, the rather quick change of position, and the way the headmistress had handled it stirred up old feelings of insecurity, mistrust, and retaliation. There was criticism and anger about the way the headmistress had coped with finding a substitute for the teacher—which had to be dealt with shortly before Christmas. Rumours arose—some of which also reached our ears. Furthermore, the leaders had at last been informed that one of the deputies was to be transferred shortly after New Year. The other deputy temporally joined the teachers in their blame of the headmistress. On top of all this, the teachers' representative had declared that he wanted to take a leave!

In the midst of this turmoil, we decided together with the headmistress that we would postpone the follow-up meeting with the whole school until the emotional climate had calmed down a little. My colleague and I decided to invite the headmistress to a talk with us alone, since we thought that her situation was very difficult. But she decided to come with her deputy, because she did not feel strong enough at the time to cope with the suspiciousness that she expected would be aroused if she met with us by herself. During this meeting with the two of them in the New Year, we wanted to explore how things were at the school, how things were for the two leaders, what they needed our help for, and what they thought the teachers expected of us.

The feedback we had was that things had calmed down considerably at the school. The two leaders had been very busy taking up new tasks after the third leader's departure. There had again been some very good meetings in the teachers' council, and there had even been renewed interest in taking up some of the ideas from the consultation weekend. There were still bad feelings about the circumstances around the teacher who had decided to leave. The headmistress felt in a very vulnerable position and could still feel the blame and the distance from the teachers—although a few of them had revealed to her that they did not agree with their colleagues.

At this meeting we were given all the details about the teacher who had decide to move to another school. It turned out to be very complicated and contained much negative "history" about the teacher, and put the headmistress in the position of having to protect both the teacher and herself at the same time. It was our impression that she had handled the whole matter very well under the given circumstances—even though she had acted a little fast, not giving time to involve the relevant teachers. Our dilemma was that we still lacked an understanding of why the teachers so readily mistrusted their headmistress. We wondered whether the reason related to something in her relationship with the teachers, or if her role as scapegoat had come about for completely other reasons. When we thought about it, we could almost see a pattern here. It seemed as though the teachers wanted perfection in their chief. Seeing faults in her stirred up their aggression. But when she did things right, there was never any positive feedback to her. We saw almost a parent–child relationship, and our guess was that the child was rather childish and had its own problems.

THE FINAL FOLLOW-UP MEETING
WITH THE WHOLE SCHOOL

The meeting with the two leaders helped us to decide that the content of this meeting should primarily be about the weekend consultation, and that we would deal with the previous conflict only if this came up. To stress this we had sent out to the staff at the school a résumé of the most important discussions and proposals for change that had come up during the weekend.

When my colleague and I were planning this follow-up meeting, we reviewed the whole consultation up till now. We tried to imagine what would be important for the school to deal with at this time, and we thought about the information and feedback we needed to go on. We also remembered the last follow-up meeting, and the way our questions had been criticized. We looked at each other and felt rather empty of ideas and new hypotheses. What came up was the feedback I had received at the final systemic consultation seminar—especially the advice to let people decide for themselves what is important for them. So, with this in mind, we finally chose to ask a few very here-and-now questions—and eventually not to have a structured plan.

We had only an afternoon for the meeting. What we did was put people in groups to discuss the following:

- "What is important to discuss now?"
- "What is unclear?"
- "What do you need to look at in your internal relations at this point?"
- "Do you think that everybody agrees about the proposals for change that came up during the consultation weekend, and what happened to them?"

When everybody formed into their subgroups, we went with the two leaders. They told us that they had been very busy reallocating the tasks of the deputy, who had left. They had put a notice on the bulletin-board about how they had allocated the tasks. Their most pressing problem was to work out the transference-list for teachers, which the headmistress was obliged to do every year. They felt that the climate at the school had calmed down. They also felt that they had been too busy, and that there had been too little time for contact with the teachers and with each other. They did not get to our questions, because it was important for the headmistress to explain some details about the transference-list situation—details that her deputy had never actually heard before. We saw this as a very important process, because it helped to clear up some of their own internal misunderstandings.

After the group discussion, we had an open discussion with a reflecting team, in which one or two groups came into the middle. Many things came up, most of which concerned the headmistress and feelings of insecurity in relation to her. When does she act, and when does she make decisions? When does she encourage and expect responsibility from the teachers? In which matters does she take the initiative and the final responsibility? People expressed feelings of insecurity and mistrust; as a consequence of such feelings, the teachers had made the decision not to speak to the headmistress alone—there had to be at least two persons! The headmistress had not been informed about this, and it came as a great surprise to her. There also were some positive comments to the two leaders about being more noticeable and more around after the third leader had left. This was interesting because the two leaders had received the opposite impression. Confusion was expressed about the teacher who had left voluntarily and about another case in which was the general opinion was that the headmistress had acted too fast without any concern for the teachers involved.

Since there were so many issues relating to the headmistress, we chose to ask her to sit with the discussion group in the middle, while the rest listened and gave feedback. After the break, we let everybody sit in the circle as one group, and we now used the time to clarify further the issues discussed. Several misunderstandings were cleared up. People admitted mistakes, and the headmistress apologized for certain of her decisions, which she could now see had been taken too fast and without thought of the consequences for certain teachers. But she also said that she was bound to make mistakes now and then, especially when under pressures of time. She wanted feedback from the teachers in such situations. We experienced greater courage among the teachers to confront the headmistress and especially greater courage to show diverging opinions among themselves. Certain incidents during the discussion even showed a willingness to contain anger and rejection.

We ended the day by stating dilemmas. We still saw the teachers' dilemma as an acceptance of lack of clarity and an unwillingness to contact the headmistress when they needed explanations or discussions. We saw the dilemma of the headmistress as a conflict between wanting to be democratic and sometimes having to make final decisions without the time to discuss these with the persons involved. Finally, my colleague stated the following intervention: "Whenever you have a problem or a conflict you could make it a habit to do the following analysis: What is the case? Who ought to be involved in the case? Write down a procedure about how you want to work with the case. Who participates in the process of decision? Who has the final responsibility?"

We experienced a relaxed, even relieved atmosphere when we finished. We sat for a little while with the leaders and a few teachers and had an informal talk about our consultation and whether our job had perhaps now come to an end.

CONCLUSION

We actually decided to have one final meeting with the whole school and one with the leaders to end the consultation.

The consultation with this school had lasted for a year and a half. Later, when my colleague and I sat down to think and talk about the process, and what we had learned from it, certain things became clear to us. We thought that the time span had been too long. The meetings and two consultation weekends had been too far apart in time. From the feedback at the meetings, we observed that people became more trained in saying things directly, in listening, and in asking questions. Our guess is that this learning process would be more effective if the time-span were shorter. It might also help people to keep the learning and their own decisions in mind if we gave them tasks in-between the consultation meetings.

We speculated about how we had helped the school. We could see the school adopting an easier way to start the meetings and to solve conflicts, but we wondered whether this learning had been "transferred" to their everyday working life. We wondered why every conflict brought up the old antagonism between the teachers and the headmistress. This antagonism had been quite clear at several of our meetings. At times it left us with a feeling that some persons or groups of persons actually wanted to keep up this antagonism. At the same time it seemed that the teachers—at least during our meetings—had become better at asking the headmistress questions and at showing her their disagreement. She in turn had been able to listen to this and to answer in a nondefensive way.

Our own learning points in relation to the school were the following. (1) It was a great help for there to be two of us in a situation with so many people. I mostly took the active part and my colleague that of the observer. That meant that he had more free energy and could observe better and in that way was able to give me valuable feedback. But sometimes he also intervened and said something extremely relevant to the group—or to me in front of the group. Sometimes we found it difficult to separate process from content, and at times became trapped in stories and into giving advice on specific issues. Here again it was an advantage for there to be two of us, because most of the time we could help each other out of this bind. (2) We learned to be better at helping people see what they were doing when they told us stories or started to argue—to stay in the meta-position. This was the hardest part! (3) We found that it was very important to take time to have our own discussions before every meeting or consultation with the school. It was important for us to empty our minds of fantasies, worries, and hypotheses so that we would have a freer approach when we met people and would also be better prepared for strange surprises. Making the plan was part of our thinking process, but we found out that we did not always have to follow it. But in this first consultation task of ours, we found that having a plan made it easier to be spontaneous and to listen openly.

Doing this consultation with a large state school gave us a great deal of experience. What we learned from this was closely connected to what I learned at the Danish seminars, which, to our great luck, went on during the same period as our consultation task. We learned especially that it is important to listen to the whole group from the start—to use their feedback right from the start, even if it is sparse. Getting started is something you do together with your "client", and it may take time. So in a way we learned to rely more on our training as psychologists and to start a consultation the same way we would do with a new client—that is, to listen, to find out who the person is, to help define the problem, and to give feedback. We learned to be better at using conflict as an instructive process on the spot. We learned that our exercises with group discussions were constructive, and that we can rely on people to generate ideas for themselves. So we will be less structured in our next task! These were ideas from the Danish seminars that we actually tested out and obtained experience from. We also learned how important it is to deal with and listen to the special problems and responsibilities of the leader. So, with this learning in mind, we look forward to our next consultation task, even though we still feel that we are in the process of learning.

Postscript

A cautionary tale:
the man who would do no harm

Henning Nielsen

O nce upon a time there was a young man who wanted to see the big wide world before he married.

On leaving home his father spoke the following words to him: "Wherever you go and whomsoever you meet, do no harm." The son promised, and his father gave him a small bag of money so that he could pay his dues—and while he was away his father would find him a bride.

They embraced each other on parting, and the father, who was not young, hid his sorrow so the son could leave—because "he who will do no harm" cannot leave a sad father.

The young man now travelled quickly out of the village and soon came to places that he had never been before.

In the fields of a big manor house the harvest was in full swing, farmhands and maids worked with bent backs, and an overseer walked among them with a stinging rod in his hand and shouted at them that they should work harder.

Just as the young man passed by on the road, a worn-out woman collapsed in the baking sun. But the overseer gave her a kick with his boot, and she got on her feet again.

The young man remembered his father's words, called the over-seer, and asked him to be lenient as he could see that the workers were sweating drops of blood, and you can't bid a human being to carry more than it can.

But the overseer, who was not an evil man, looked at him with regret and explained that he only did what the lord of the manor demanded, and he dared not do anything else, for fear of his livelihood.

It now dawned upon the young man that he couldn't help any of them without harming the other, and as he would do no harm he left the place without having accomplished his goal.

Soon after, he got into the habit of keeping his eyes on the road, without looking to the sides, where he might see people working in the fields and forests.

Late one night he came to an inn, which was run by a widow with many children and lots to do. Yet it appeared to the young man that she was always happy, singing while she was working.

"Why are you singing when you have so many burdens to carry?", he asked. "Because singing makes my burdens lighter", she answered, which was the truth.

That night he got a place beside her in the bed, as she was always a hospitable woman. In the morning when he asked her what he owed her she answered: "What I have given you has no price." But the young man misunderstood her and his bag emptied of money, and he went off in a good mood with a new open view on the world.

There was an old coalmine at the roadside and a shift of miners were on their way down the mineshaft when the young man passed by, and he had never seen so many bowed figures and black, sad faces at one and the same time.

"Don't go down the mine", he was warned by someone who thought that he had come to look for work, "It's a short cut to hell." But the young man who would do no harm went to see the mine owner to speak to him.

"Your workers get ill when they go down the mine", he said, "It's like a short cut to hell."

The mine owner was not pleased to hear this. But he sensed what the young man meant, without quite knowing what he could do about it.

"By singing and playing music you can make heavy burdens lighter, and everybody will benefit by it", the young man said. The mine owner believed in his good intentions, if not in his words, and sent for the best flute player from the town, a fine and brilliant musician who played only in fashionable circles. He consented to let wonderful melodies stream down the shaft, as an accompaniment to the workers song, and before long the wagons with coal came up from the depths with astonishing speed.

But, alas, it lasted for only a brief time. Every time the workers raised their voices in the narrow tunnels, they breathed in large amounts of coal dust, and the song that could make heavy burdens lighter was soon replaced by painful fits of coughing. "Who are you that you can speak about what is good for us", one worker said with a face distorted with rage, when he came up the shaft—the very same worker who had previously warned him against a short cut to hell.

"I am here to do no harm", the young man said, "but I now see that I have made a mistake".

But the mine owner thanked the young man for his efforts and thought that it was better than doing nothing just to have done something. And as a proof of his gratitude he gave the young man a shining silver coin, which was, after all, a godsend, as he had already given away everything that his father had given him.

After that he kept as far away from other people as possible, and slept in outhouses and haystacks while he thought the matter over. He had experienced that it was no easy matter to do no harm without harming anybody. He now understood that you must be cautious helping anybody who has not asked for it—maybe it will be somebody else who will thank you for it.

When he came to a huge sea port with many people and ships it was with some hesitation that he entered the port.

Down in the port there was a large crowd gathered around an old sailor with a big, richly coloured parrot on his shoulder. But most impressive of all was the parrot's talent for imitating voices, and people gladly threw a few pennies into the sailor's cap to hear the parrot answer them in exactly their own voice. What a lucky parrot, which does no harm, the young man sighed.

Now, there was a rich merchant who lived in the town, and he owned many ships, offices, and property, but he scared people with his unpredictable temper and he was, therefore, also very lonely.

Every evening he sat on his balcony and looked out onto the port and the sea, where his ships came sailing. And he sighed loudly from his loneliness, so loudly that people all over the town could hear it, but none dared do anything about it.

But the young man, who didn't know better, placed himself below the balcony and heaved a deep sigh in a voice that could hardly be distinguished from the merchant's own.

When the merchant heard this he at first got very angry but when he leaned out over the balcony to scold the wag he looked down into the young man's dauntless face and invited him in instead.

Every night they sat on the balcony and talked about the sorrows and disappointments of the merchant, about the day that was gone and the day that was coming.

Now, the fact was this: that the merchant was a complicated man who neither liked to be contradicted nor always to be echoed and told of the correctness of his view. But the young man soon perceived this and learned to master the art of answering the merchant in such a way that it was both different and yet the same.

And if nothing more happened, at least the sighing of the merchant was no longer heard all over the town—yes, there were those who actually missed just a sigh now and then from the balcony.

"But this can surely do no harm", the young man thought and was pleased.

Soon it was known far and wide that there was a young man with wonderful skills who understood everybody and could speak with anybody. He could answer those who consulted him in any vocal pitch, and what he said was always new, and yet the same. It was said that on a good day you would become quite dizzy not knowing who was really speaking. Yes, there were people who afterwards believed that he had not even been there and that they had invented it all themselves.

Time went on as time is in the habit of doing, and one day the young man knocked on his father's door.

When the father, now being very old, weak, and with bad hearing, saw his son again his eyes filled with tears. "I can see that your bag of money is bigger than the one I gave you on the way", he said, "but whether or not you have paid everyone their dues in all these years, I don't know".

And the son got his bride, a girl so delightful, with long, flowing locks, almond-shaped eyes, and a heart of gold.

Soon they became a small family, and every day the young man brought his wife gifts and said the sweetest words to her.

However, it was as though he always spoke with strange voices—and every time he opened his mouth it was a new voice that spoke, but never his own.

But as he didn't notice it himself—and his wife wondered but had never known him to be any different—none could, with certainty, say that they didn't live happily.

REFERENCES

Andersen, T. (1990). *The Reflecting Team*. New York; W. W. Norton.

Anderson, H., Goolishian, H., & Winderman, L. (1986). Problem-determined systems: towards transformation in family therapy. *Journal of Strategic and Systemic Therapies, 5*: 1-13.

Argyris, C. (1990). *Overcoming Organizational Defenses*. London: Allyn & Bacon.

Campbell, D., Coldicott, T., & Kinsella, K. (1994). *Systemic Work with Organizations: A New Model for Managers and Change*. London: Karnac Books.

Campbell, D., Draper, R., & Huffington, C. (1991). *A Systemic Approach to Consultation*. London: Karnac Books.

Drucker, P. (1990). *Managing the Non-Profit Organisation*. Oxford: Butterworth-Heinemann.

Fruggeri, L., & McNamee, S. (1991). Burnout as social process: a research study. In: L. Fruggeri et al., *New Systemic Ideas from the Italian Mental Health Movement*. London: Karnac Books.

Hampden-Turner, C. (1990). *Charting the Corporate Mind*. Oxford: Blackwell.

Huffington, C., & Brunning, H. (1994). *Internal Consultancy in the Public Sector: Case Studies*. London: Karnac Books.

Jenner, Håkan, & Segraeus, Vera (Eds.) (1989). *Att hålla lågan levande. Om bemästrande av utbrändthet.* Lund: Student-litteratur.

Lazarus, R. S., & Folkman, S. (1984). Coping and adaption. In: W. D. Gentry (Ed.), *Handbook of Behavioral Medicine.* New York: Guilford Press.

Maslach, C. (1982). *Burnout. The Cost of Caring.* Englewood Cliffs, NJ: Prentice-Hall.

McCaughan, N., & Palmer, B. (1994). *Systems Thinking for Harassed Managers.* London: Karnac Books.

Morgan, G. (1986). *Images of Organization.* Newbury, CA: Sage.

Rasmussen, N. H. (1990). Psykisk arbejdsmiljø. In: S. E. Christensen (Ed.), *Dig og dit arbejdsmiljø. Om arbejdsmiljøet i social og sundhedsektoren. Temabog for social- og sundhedsområdet.* Copenhagen: HAF/DKA og Dafolo.

Schein, E. (1987). *Process Consultation, Vol. 2.* Reading, MA: Addison-Wesley.

Selvini Palazzoli, M., et al. (1986). *Hidden Games in Organizations.* New York: Pantheon Books.

Senge, P. (1990). *The Fifth Discipline.* New York: Doubleday.

Wynne, L., McDaniel, S., & Weber, T. (Eds.) (1986). *Systems Consultation. A New Perspective for Family Therapy.* New York: Guilford Press.

APPPENDIX A

Recommended reading list for the Danish seminars

Andersen, T. (1990). *The Reflecting Team*. New York: W. W. Norton.

Anderson, H., & Goolishian, H. (1988). Human systems as linguistic systems: preliminary and evolving ideas about the implications for clinical theory. *Family Process, 27* (4): 371–384.

Anderson, H., Goolishian, H., & Winderman, L. (1986). Problem-determined systems: towards transformation in family therapy. *Journal of Strategic and Systemic Therapies, 5*: 1-13.

Argyris, C. (1990). *Overcoming Organizational Defenses*. London: Allyn & Bacon.

Bateson, G. (1973). *Steps to an Ecology of Mind*. London: Paladin.

Campbell, D., Coldicott, T., & Kinsella, K. (1994). *Systemic Work with Organizations*. London: Karnac Books.

Campbell, D., Draper, R., & Huffington, C. (1991a). *A Systemic Approach to Consultation*. London: Karnac Books.

Campbell, D., Draper, R., & Huffington, C. (1991b). *Teaching Systemic Thinking*. London: Karnac Books.

Drucker, P. (1990). *Managing the Non-Profit Organisation*. Oxford: Butterworth-Heinemann.

Gergen, K. (1985). The social constructionist movement in modern psychology. *American Psychologist, 40*: 266–275.

155

Hampden-Turner, C. (1990). *Charting the Corporate Mind.* Oxford: Blackwell.

Huffington, C., & Brunning, H. (1994). *Internal Consultancy in the Public Sector: Case Studies.* London: Karnac Books.

Keeney, B. P. (1983). *Aesthetics of Change.* New York: Guilford Press.

Maturana, H., & Varela, F. (1980). *Autopoiesis and Cognition.* Dordrecht: Reidel.

McCaughan, N., & Palmer, B. (1994). *Systems Thinking for Harassed Managers.* London: Karnac Books.

Morgan, G. (1986). *Images of Organization.* Newbury, CA: Sage.

Morgan, G. (1988). *Riding the Waves of Change: Developing Managerial Competencies for a Turbulent World.* San Francisco, CA: Jossey-Bass.

Schein, E. (1987). *Process Consultation, Vol. 2.* Reading, MA: Addison-Wesley.

Selvini Palazzoli, M., Boscolo, L., Cecchin, G., & Prata, G. (1970). *Paradox and counterparadox.* New York: Jason Aronson.

Selvini Palazzoli, M., et al., 1986. *Hidden Games in Organizations.* New York: Pantheon Books.

Senge, P. (1990). *The Fifth Discipline.* New York: Doubleday.

Shotter, J., & Gergen, K. (Eds.) (1989). *Texts of Identity.* London: Sage.

Von Foerster, H. (1981). *Observing Systems.* Seaside, CA: Intersystems Publications.

Von Glasersfeld, E. (1984). An introduction to radical constructionism. In: P. Watzlawick (Ed.), *The Invented Reality.* New York: W. W. Norton

Watzlawick, P., Weakland, J., & Fisch, R. (1974). *Change.* New York: W. W. Norton.

White, M. (1991). *Deconstruction and Therapy.* Dulwich Centre Newsletter, No. 3. Adelaide: Dulwich Centre.

Wynne, L., McDaniel, S., & Weber, T. (Eds.) (1986). *Systems Consultation. A New Perspective for Family Therapy.* London: Guilford Press.

APPENDIX B

Participants in the Danish seminars

Kirsten Agerskov
Hanne Kold Andersen
Dodo Astrup
Vivi Bech
Inger Dræby
Jan Fjordbak
Jytte Gandløse
Janne Graff
Anders Groth
Hannah Gulbrandsen
Ken Vagn Hansen
Mette Riis Hansen
Gitte Haslebo
Birgitte Holst
Grith Ingvorsen
Hans Kærbo

Irene Kejser
Nini Leick
Nikolaj Lunøe
Flemming Madsen
Kirsten Muus
Bodil Nejsum
Henning Nielsen
Jan F. Nielsen
Bodil Pedersen
Johnny Petersen
Berit Sander
Kirsten Skafte
Birgit Søderberg
Ole Michael Spaten
Henning Strand
Hanne Winsløw

INDEX